Elevate ˙

Copyright © 2023

This book is sold with the understanding that the author and publisher are not engaged in rendering any specific professional or expert advice. The information provided in this book is for educational and entertainment purposes only. The reader is advised to seek appropriate professional advice before making any decision.

ISBN : 9798864747223
First edition, 2023

Index

Ignite Your Leadership Journey..4

Day 1 - Collective Leadership: The Teamwork Edge...................................6

Day 2 - The Essence of True Leadership...15

Day 4 - Game-Changing Strategies for Workplace Empowerment.....35

Day 5 - Embrace Disagreements for a Thriving Work Culture.............45

Day 6 - Good vs Bad Leadership 55

Day 7 - Redefining Leadership Beyond Titles and Ranks.......................66

Day 8 - The Power of Trust in Leadership 76

Day 9 - Choosing the Right Circle of Influence...86

Day 10 - Why Employee Turnover is Your Wake-Up Call 96

Day 11 - Conquer Challenges and Step Out of Your Comfort Zone...107

Day 12 - Positive Leadership: A Catalyst for Success...............................117

Day 13 - Turn Your Business into a Thriving Family...............................127

Day 14 - Lead with Character, Transform Your World...........................137

Day 15 - Modern Leadership...148

Day 16 - The Power of Integrity and Character 158

Day 17 - Dual Nature of Leadership..168

Day 18 - The Power of Appreciating Team Members in Tough Times
179

Day 19 - Supportive Leadership 189

Day 20 - The Shift from Followers to Leaders in Organizational
Excellence 199

Day 21 - Empowering Leadership..209

Day 22 - Transforming Toxic Workplaces 219

Day 23 - Influence in a Changing World..230

Day 24 - Real Leadership 241

Day 25 - Empathy for Transformative Leadership 251

Day 26 - Proven Strategies for Transformative Impact.........................261

Day 27 - Resilience and Personal Growth..272

Day 28 - The Transformative Power of Inspirational Leadership...281

Day 29 - Purpose, Passion, and the Power to Transform......................292

Day 30 - Altruism and Generosity..303

Embracing the Leadership Horizon...314

Ignite Your Leadership Journey

Welcome, aspiring leader, to a journey that promises transformation and growth. Every step, every challenge, every lesson ahead is designed to ignite that latent spark within you, turning it into a blazing trail of influence and inspiration. "Elevate Your Leadership: A 30-Day Challenge" is not just a title; it's a call to action, beckoning you to rise higher, dream bigger, and lead with unparalleled passion.

Leadership is not just about authority or a title. It's about impact, influence, and the ability to inspire change, even in the face of adversity. It's about understanding that every interaction, every decision, and every action has the potential to shape the world around us. Over the next 30 days, you will be given tools, insights, and challenges that will push you out of your comfort zone and into the realm of true leadership.

But remember, transformation doesn't occur overnight. It's a journey, a process, and sometimes, it demands patience, resilience, and an unwavering belief in oneself. As you embark on this 30-day challenge, there may be moments of doubt, moments when the climb feels steep. But in those moments, I urge you to reflect on your 'why' – the reason you picked up this book, the vision you have for yourself, and the change you wish to see in the world.

Your potential is boundless, and the world is in dire need of visionary leaders who lead with empathy, integrity, and purpose. So, as you turn each page, immerse yourself fully, engage with each exercise, and commit to the process. The road to leadership excellence is paved with dedication, introspection, and continuous learning.

I want to remind you of a simple truth: Leadership is a journey, not a destination. And like any journey, it's the experiences, the growth, and the connections we make along the way that truly matter. So, gear up, embrace the challenge, and let's elevate your leadership together. Your future awaits, and it looks incredibly bright.

Day 1 - Collective Leadership: The Teamwork Edge

"To build a strong team, you must see someone else's strength as a complement to your weakness, and not a threat to your position or authority" - Christine Caine

In the world of business, great leadership isn't about one person's success; it's about the combined wisdom of the whole team. It's a common misconception to attribute success solely to the leader when, in reality, it is the amalgamation of ideas, efforts, and expertise of every team member that propels a venture forward. A singular genius might spark a flame, but it takes the combined efforts of many to keep the fire burning.

Effective leaders understand the profound power of listening. They do not dominate conversations, believing their vision to be the sole path forward. Instead, they are curious and inquisitive, asking questions and genuinely valuing the responses. By fostering an environment where every team member feels heard and encouraged to contribute, leaders harness a spectrum of insights, leading to richer strategies and more informed decisions.

The mark of a true leader isn't trying to wear every hat but recognizing who wears each hat best. By entrusting tasks to those best suited for them, a leader not only optimizes productivity but also ensures that they can focus on their paramount responsibilities. This delegation is not a sign of relinquishing control, but rather a strategic move to elevate the entire team's potential.

Humility, often overlooked, is a cornerstone of great leadership. In business, leaders who stand out are those who do not let their egos dictate their actions. They recognize that they are not infallible, and rather than shying away from their mistakes, they embrace them as learning opportunities. Such leaders are not threatened by the expertise of others but are eager to learn and grow from it.

Remember that true leadership isn't about standing alone on a pedestal, but rather about walking hand in hand with those around you. Embrace the power of collective wisdom, for in the chorus of diverse voices and shared aspirations, you'll discover the true melody of success. It's not the lone wolf, but the harmonious pack that shapes the future.

And as you journey forward, let humility be your compass and active listening your map. By valuing the contributions of each individual, you're not just building a successful venture, but cultivating a community rooted in trust and mutual respect. **Remember, that in unity, we find not just strength, but also the profound magic of collective potential.**

Three Insightful Questions to Ponder on This Topic

Do you ensure everyone in your team feel valued or often dismiss their opinions?

Active listening is a crucial skill for effective leadership. When you realize that dominating conversations, it may be time to take a step back and allow others to share their perspectives. Begin meetings with open-ended questions and encourage diverse viewpoints. Listen more than you speak, and when you do respond, ensure it is with understanding and empathy. Over time, you'll find that by valuing the input of all team members, you cultivate an environment of trust, respect, and innovation. Remember, the best leaders aren't always the loudest voices in the room, but rather those who can harness the collective wisdom of their teams.

When things go wrong, do you defend yourself or learn from your experience?

Humility is a hallmark of great leadership. If you find yourself constantly defending your actions or decisions, it might be due to an inflated ego or fear of appearing weak. However, the most respected leaders are those who admit their mistakes, learn from them, and seek advice when needed. By showing vulnerability and a willingness to learn, you not only enhance your own skills and understanding but also inspire those around you to be open and collaborative. Embrace challenges as growth opportunities and remember that every mistake is a lesson in disguise.

Do you micromanage or trust others with tasks they are skilled at?

Delegation is not about relinquishing control, but rather about optimizing the strengths and talents of your team. If you're trying to manage everything yourself, you're likely spreading yourself too thin and may not be allowing team members to fully utilize their expertise. Start by assessing the strengths and skills of your team members. Entrust tasks based on these strengths, providing clear expectations and the necessary resources. By doing so, you not only increase productivity but also empower your team, building their confidence and commitment to the project. Remember, true leadership is about elevating the entire team's potential, not showcasing individual prowess.

Three Actionable Insights

Foster Open Communication:

✓ Create an environment where team members feel safe to voice their opinions, ideas, and concerns. This can be achieved through regular team meetings, feedback sessions, and one-on-one check-ins.

✓ Dedicate a portion of team meetings for open discussions. Encourage team members to share their insights and ensure that everyone has an equal opportunity to speak. Consider using tools like anonymous suggestion boxes or feedback platforms to gather uninhibited opinions.

Empower Through Delegation:

✓ Recognize the strengths and expertise of each team member and assign tasks accordingly. This not only optimizes efficiency but also boosts the confidence and ownership of team members.

✓ Regularly review the skills and passions of your team members. Assign roles and tasks based on their strengths. Provide the necessary training and resources to help them excel in their assigned roles.

Cultivate a Learning Environment:

✓ Embrace mistakes as learning opportunities. Instead of penalizing errors, focus on what can be learned and how to improve in the future.

✓ When errors occur, gather the team to discuss the root causes and brainstorm solutions. Celebrate the lessons learned and encourage a growth mindset by sharing resources, workshops, and training opportunities.

Personal Notes

_____

_____

_____

_____

_____

_____

_____

_____

_____

_____

_____

_____

_____

Day 2 - The Essence of True Leadership

"Never look down on anybody unless you're helping them up." - Jesse Jackson

Too often, in the bustling corridors of power and the echoing halls of prestige, leadership is misconstrued as merely holding a revered title. But ask yourself, is leadership merely about having your name engraved on a plaque or on the door of a corner office? No, true leadership is about diving deep into the sea of potential and bringing out the pearls from within your team. It's about helping your people shine, helping your team soar, and helping individuals discover the strength they never knew they possessed.

"Leaders become great not because of their power, but because of their ability to empower others." This poignant quote by John Maxwell encapsulates the very essence of what leadership should stand for. It's not the crown you wear but the legacy you leave behind, not the accolades you accumulate but the lives you positively transform. Every time you help someone climb a step higher, you've exhibited the very core of leadership.

Understand that leadership is more than just a title. It's a tremendous responsibility, an art of nurturing, guiding, and fostering growth. The mantle of leadership isn't just about guiding people but about helping people navigate their own paths. When you lead, remember that every word you speak, every action you take, has the potential to either uplift or tear down. Choose wisely.

Helping your people, helping your team, helping individuals to find their footing in this vast world – that's the true calling of a leader. It's not about standing at the pinnacle alone but ensuring that everyone you're responsible for reaches their own summits. Leadership, at its core, is a selfless journey where the destination is not your own success but the success of those you lead.

So, as you walk the path of leadership, recognize the gravity of the influence you wield. It's not about the title you hold but the hands you hold out to lift others. Remember, in every interaction, in every decision, you have the power to change lives. Lead with compassion, with purpose, and with the unwavering commitment to helping your people reach the zenith of their potential.

In life, it's easy to get caught up in titles, thinking they define our value. But I urge you to look beyond these fleeting symbols of status. True leadership, the kind that resonates and leaves a lasting mark, isn't found in titles or accolades. It's found in the silent moments when you uplift someone from their darkest depths, when you ignite a spark in someone who's lost their way, or when you simply believe in someone more than they believe in themselves. Every time you extend your hand to help, every time you inspire someone to reach a bit higher, you embody the essence of genuine leadership.

Remember, it's not about standing in the spotlight; it's about shining a light on others, guiding them towards their destined path. Your true legacy as a leader won't be measured by the titles you've held but by the hearts you've touched and the lives you've transformed. **Embrace this profound responsibility and wear it as a badge of honor. For in the end, the true measure of leadership is not where you stand, but who stands taller because of you.**

Three Insightful Questions to Ponder on This Topic

Are you leading to uplift others or chasing personal glory?

True leadership isn't about personal aggrandizement. If your primary motivation is to gain personal recognition or to collect accolades, you may find your influence waning over time. People can sense when a leader is genuine in their intent and when they are self-serving. To truly progress in leadership, shift your focus from "I" to "We." Celebrate team successes more than personal ones. When you empower those around you, not only do you elevate the entire team, but you also solidify your position as a genuine leader. Remember, leadership is less about the leader and more about those being led. Invest in their growth, provide them with opportunities, and recognize their achievements. In doing so, you'll find that your own success and recognition will naturally follow.

How can you inspire your team with your words and actions without discouraging them?

Communication is a powerful tool in the hands of a leader. Every word you utter and every action you take has a ripple effect on your team and organization. To ensure that you're uplifting and inspiring, practice active listening. By truly listening to your team, you can gauge their needs, concerns, and aspirations. This will help you tailor your communication in a way that resonates and motivates. Additionally, seek feedback. Encourage an open environment where team members feel safe to express their thoughts about your leadership style. By understanding how your words and actions are perceived, you can make necessary adjustments. Always remember, a leader's true strength isn't in dictating but in facilitating a culture of trust, growth, and mutual respect.

Are titles more important to you than actual leadership qualities?

Titles and accolades can be gratifying, but they are fleeting and often external markers of success. What endures is the impact you have on individuals, the growth you foster, and the positive changes you effect. Whenever you detect overly concerned with titles or external recognition, take a step back and re-evaluate your priorities. Engage with your team on a personal level, understand their aspirations, challenges, and dreams. By immersing yourself in the actual work of leadership, you'll find a deeper and more fulfilling sense of purpose. Remember, the most revered leaders aren't always the ones with the loftiest titles but those who leave a lasting, positive mark on the lives of those they lead. Prioritize people over prestige, and you'll find your leadership journey to be far more rewarding and impactful.

Three Actionable Insights

Focus on Impact, Not Recognition:

✓ Instead of seeking validation through titles or promotions, concentrate on the tangible impact you're making. Assess your contributions by the positive changes they bring about, whether that's streamlining a process, mentoring a colleague, or delivering an important project.

✓ Weekly, jot down the positive impacts you've made, no matter how small, and reflect on their significance without tying them to a title.

Build Authentic Relationships:

✓ Genuine connections are built on trust and mutual respect, not titles. Prioritize building relationships where you can both offer and seek guidance, irrespective of hierarchies.

✓ Make it a point to connect with colleagues from various levels in your organization.

Organize or participate in team-building activities, and be open to feedback from all.

Practice Humility:

✓ Titles can inflate egos, but true leaders remain grounded. Recognize the contributions of others and understand that every role, regardless of title, plays a crucial part in the success of an organization.

✓ Celebrate team successes publicly, acknowledging everyone involved. When recognized for your work, share the credit with those who helped you.

Personal Notes

Day 3 - Unleash Your Potential, Don't Diminish Your Light

"Not everything that is faced can be changed, but nothing can be changed until it is faced." - James Baldwin

You're on this Earth for a reason. Never minimize yourself to fit the mold that society or anyone else tries to force upon you. You are not a square peg meant to fit into a round hole. You are a unique blend of talents, dreams, and capabilities, designed to accomplish great things. Don't let the world tame you into an unremarkable version of yourself.

People might tell you to tread softly, to limit your aspirations, to color inside the lines. Don't listen. They do this because they're afraid of the light that shines within you, the light that has the power to unsettle, to revolutionize, to lead. When you're told to "be realistic," understand that you're being asked to become smaller, to stunt your growth. Don't become a shadow of your potential self.

Instead, unleash your power. Invest in your personal growth and self-empowerment. Read voraciously. Learn continuously. Challenge yourself daily. The more you grow, the more you realize how limitless your potential truly is. There's an incredible version of you that's waiting to be discovered. Go find it.

In this journey, you will encounter resistance. Not everyone will understand your quest for personal growth. They may call you obsessive, intense, or even selfish. Don't let this deter you. These voices come from those who have settled, and they find your ambition confronting. Your growth is not a mirror for their inadequacies—it's a testament to your courage.

Your life is your masterpiece, a one-of-a-kind tapestry of experiences and achievements. Make it as vibrant, as grand, and as compelling as you can. Because the truth is, the world doesn't need more people who are content with mediocrity. What the world needs is more trailblazers, more innovators, more leaders—more individuals like the person you're becoming.

Listen up, my friend! You've got a fire in you that's just waiting to roar. Don't ever think you need to dim that light to fit into some mold society wants to shove you into. You're not a carbon copy; you're an original masterpiece, with your own set of skills, dreams, and untapped potential. When people tell you to "tone it down" or "be realistic," what they're really saying is, "Your greatness scares me." Don't let anyone's insecurities snuff out your flame.

Now, I want you to focus on leveling up. Personal growth isn't a luxury; it's a necessity for the life you're meant to lead. Imagine the strongest, most empowered version of yourself—now understand that even that is just a stepping stone to how incredible you can really be. Take risks, read, learn, fail, and get back up again. **Challenge yourself to be a little better each day, because the world doesn't just need "okay" or "good enough." The world** needs the awe-inspiring, trailblazing YOU. So go out there and show 'em what you're made of!

Three Insightful Questions to Ponder on This Topic

Do you downplay your dreams due to fear of criticism?

It's natural to seek validation and acceptance from those around us, but it's crucial to recognize when this desire hinders our true potential. Should it occur to you that frequently downplaying your dreams or changing your course due to fear of criticism, it's time to introspect. Understand that every great leader, innovator, or trailblazer faced criticism at some point. Instead of letting fear dictate your choices, seek alignment with your true self. Surround yourself with positive, like-minded individuals who support and uplift your dreams. Remember, your unique path is what sets you apart and could potentially lead to your greatest achievements.

Are you actively pursuing personal growth, or are you remaining too comfortable?

Personal growth doesn't always come easy. It demands time, effort, and stepping out of one's comfort zone. If you feel like you're stagnating, it's essential to take proactive steps. Set aside dedicated time for self-improvement activities like reading, learning new skills, or attending workshops. Challenge yourself with tasks that you've previously avoided. Embrace failures as learning opportunities, not setbacks. Remember, every day offers a chance to grow, and by pushing your boundaries, you inch closer to realizing the limitless potential within you.

Do you fully grasp the criticisms that may be hindering your personal growth?

While it's essential to stay true to your path, it's also valuable to occasionally assess the criticisms or feedback you receive. Sometimes, these voices might be coming from a place of concern or genuine feedback. Distinguish between constructive feedback and criticism rooted in others' insecurities or fears. Once you can discern the difference, you'll be better equipped to address genuine concerns while sidestepping negativity that aims to pull you down. Always remember, your journey is personal to you, and while it's good to listen, the final choices should resonate with your inner voice and aspirations.

Three Actionable Insights

Set Boundaries and Prioritize Self-Care:

In a world that glorifies busyness, it's easy to forget the importance of self-care. Understand that working yourself to the bone isn't a sustainable path to success; it's a one-way ticket to burnout. Set clear boundaries—know when to say no to additional responsibilities that don't align with your goals or contribute to your growth. Schedule time for self-care, be it through exercise, mindfulness, or pursuing a hobby. When you're well-rested and mentally sharp, you'll be more effective, creative, and a better leader in the workplace.

Leverage Your Unique Strengths:

Everyone has a unique set of skills and talents that they bring to the table—these are your superpowers. Do a self-assessment to figure out what these are. It could be your ability to think critically, your knack for problem-solving, or your exceptional interpersonal skills. Once you've identified them, find ways to leverage these strengths in your daily tasks and projects. Don't just stick to your job description; go above and beyond by applying your unique strengths to add value in ways that only you can. This not only makes you invaluable but also creates a sense of fulfillment and empowerment.

Set Stretch Goals and Monitor Progress:
"Good enough" should never be good enough for you. Always aim higher. Set goals that make you stretch beyond your comfort zone. These shouldn't be impossible, but they should require you to grow, learn, and adapt. Break these stretch goals down into smaller, achievable tasks, and monitor your progress regularly. Celebrate the small wins, but also take time to analyze setbacks or failures for the lessons they offer. This iterative process of setting challenging objectives and tracking your advancement creates a cycle of continuous personal growth and keeps you motivated.

Personal Notes

Day 4 - Game-Changing Strategies for Workplace Empowerment

"Go where your effort is appreciated. Don't let your actions go unnoticed by individuals who are never satisfied"- Billy Chapata

Never underestimate the power of your own self-worth. You are an incredible force, capable of achieving great things and turning the world around you into a place overflowing with opportunities. Recognize your value; you are not a number on a scale, a grade on a paper, or a title on a business card. You are a unique blend of talents, passions, and experiences that no one else can replicate.

Never allow anyone to define who you are. The moment you let others' judgments cloud your own perception of yourself, you give away your personal power. Understand that people who belittle you or undermine your potential often do so because of their own insecurities. Take back control of your self-image, and you'll find a reservoir of untapped strength and capabilities within.

Never settle for mediocrity when you were designed for greatness. Extraordinary lives are not built on complacency; they're constructed through a relentless pursuit of excellence. Don't just aim to get by—aim to excel. In every situation, ask yourself, "Is this the best I can do?" If the answer is no, push harder. Greatness is not an accident; it's a choice.

Never let fear or doubt dictate your actions. These are the enemies of personal empowerment, the dark clouds that obscure the radiant sun of your potential. Face your fears, challenge your doubts, and turn them into stepping stones on your path to success. Remember, every risk you don't take is a guarantee of a life of ordinariness.

And finally, never forget that the world is a place teeming with opportunities. Your life can be as extraordinary and fulfilling as you make it. Take charge, seize opportunities, and cultivate an abundant life. The power to live an extraordinary life lies within you—unleash it, and you'll realize that the world isn't just something you live in; it's something you make.

Listen, you are a powerhouse of untapped potential just waiting to burst forth. Don't let anyone ever tell you otherwise! You're not just a cog in the machine; you're the whole darn engine, fueled by a unique blend of talents and passions that only you possess. It's time you recognize your own value, shake off the shackles of other people's judgments, and own your personal power. Say it with me: "I am capable of greatness!"

But let's get real. Greatness doesn't come from sitting on the sidelines; it comes from diving into life headfirst. You've got to push past the fear, the doubt, and especially the critics. They don't define you; you define you. So go ahead, take risks, aim high, and never settle for mediocrity. Your life is a canvas of endless possibilities—grab the brush and paint yourself an extraordinary and fulfilling masterpiece.

You owe it to yourself, and the world deserves to see what you've got!

Three Insightful Questions to Ponder on This Topic

Do external opinions define your worth?

External factors, whether it's societal pressures, peer opinions, or even media portrayals, can deeply influence our self-perception. If you find yourself valuing your worth based on external opinions, it's crucial to reconnect with your intrinsic value. Start by maintaining a journal where you note down your achievements, however small they might be. This isn't just about big wins but also about personal growth, kindness, resilience, and more. Over time, this journal will serve as a tangible reminder of your unique value. Also, consider limiting exposure to negative influences and surrounding yourself with supportive and positive individuals who uplift you.

Are you avoiding risks and limiting your growth?

Fear and doubt are natural emotions, but succumbing to them can stall your progress. Start by identifying specific fears or doubts that hold you back. Once identified, confront them head-on. For example, if you're afraid of public speaking, join a group like Toastmasters to practice and improve. If it's fear of failure, remember that every setback provides a lesson, and every success story has its fair share of failures. Begin with small risks and gradually move to bigger challenges as you build confidence. Celebrate each victory, and learn from each setback. This iterative process will help reduce the power of fear and doubt over time.

Are you aiming for excellence or settling?

Striving for excellence doesn't mean seeking perfection; it means giving your best effort in every situation. Begin by setting clear and measurable goals for yourself in different areas of your life – be it professional, personal, or even hobbies. Regularly evaluate your progress towards these goals. If by chance you stumble upon. falling into complacency, remember the vision you have for your life. Seek mentorship or guidance from individuals who excel in areas you're passionate about. Their insights and experiences can rekindle your motivation. Remember, the pursuit of excellence is a continuous journey, so be patient and persistent.

Three Actionable Insights

Set Micro-Goals for Macro-Impact:

One of the best ways to recognize your own value and potential is to set small, achievable goals that contribute to larger objectives at work. Instead of getting overwhelmed by a big project or long-term goals, break them down into manageable tasks. Each time you accomplish one, give yourself credit. This not only boosts your sense of self-worth but also makes the path to greatness more achievable. It's like building a skyscraper; you don't start with the 100th floor. You lay a strong foundation and build up, one level at a time.

Implement a 'No Negativity' Zone:

Negative influences can come in many forms: gossip, constant criticism, or even self-doubt. To foster personal empowerment, make a conscious decision to avoid these energy-draining activities and mindsets. If a conversation starts to go negative, steer it back to something constructive or excuse yourself. Likewise, when self-doubt creeps in, counteract it with positive affirmations or factual evidence of your past achievements. By keeping negativity at bay, you'll create a mental space that encourages growth and happiness.

Be Your Own Advocate:

In a work environment, your skills and contributions might not always be immediately recognized. Waiting for external validation can be disheartening and detrimental to your sense of self-worth. Instead, take the initiative to showcase your value. Whether it's by volunteering for projects where you can shine, or by periodically updating your supervisor about your accomplishments in a non-bragging manner, make sure people are aware of your contributions. Being your own advocate doesn't mean being arrogant; it's about giving yourself the platform you deserve.

Personal Notes

Day 5 - Embrace Disagreements for a Thriving Work Culture

"Good leadership requires you to surround yourself with people of diverse perspectives who can disagree with you without fear of retaliation."- Doris Kearns Goodwin

In a really strong team, disagreements aren't mistakes or problems; they're the secret sauce that helps everyone grow and come up with amazing ideas. Too often, traditional work environments celebrate a false harmony, where consensus is valued over constructive conflict. This mindset not only stymies growth but also fosters a culture of complacency. In such settings, one has to ask, is the team really united or merely avoiding the discomfort that comes with disagreement? Just imagine an orchestra where every musician played the same note; the end result would be far from harmonious, lacking the depth and complexity that make music, well, musical.

The reluctance to embrace differing opinions stems from a misguided notion that uniformity equates to unity. In reality, this creates an echo chamber that stifles creativity and innovation. Why do we fear the tension that comes with differing viewpoints? Could it be that we've conflated respectful debate with disunity? The most groundbreaking ideas often arise from the furnace of constructive conflict. It is through the crucible of varied perspectives and healthy debate that raw concepts are refined into transformative solutions.

So, what should an ideal work environment look like? Picture a table where everyone has a seat and every voice is valued. At this table, disagreements are not just tolerated; they are encouraged. The leader's role here is not to be the loudest voice but the most attentive ear. It's about fostering a culture where team members feel empowered to express their thoughts without fear of ridicule or reprisal. This open environment is where creativity flourishes, leading to better decision-making and problem-solving.

But creating such a culture doesn't happen overnight. It begins with leadership that is open to self-examination and willing to challenge the status quo. Are you, as a leader, setting the example by seeking out diverse opinions? Are you creating a safe space where team members can speak openly? If not, then it's time to become the catalyst for this cultural shift. It's up to you to set the tone, to show that it's not just okay to disagree—it's expected.

Hey there, you incredible force of nature! Listen up, because this is crucial: disagreement isn't your enemy; it's your ally on the road to greatness. You see, when you're in a room where everyone agrees with you, you're not in a room that's growing—you're in a comfort zone. And let's be real, nothing groundbreaking ever happened in a comfort zone. If you're leading a team or part of one, be the game-changer who invites different perspectives to the table. Understand this—every time someone challenges your idea, they're offering you a ticket to explore new angles, to dig deeper, and to come up with something even more amazing.

So, what are you waiting for? Rip up that old playbook that says uniformity equals unity. It doesn't! Unity comes from embracing each other's unique viewpoints and hammering out something extraordinary from the forge of respectful debate. Be the kind of leader, the kind of team member, the kind of human being who doesn't just tolerate differences but celebrates them. Don't settle for the safe path; blaze a trail that includes the twists and turns of diverse opinions. Because at the end of that winding road, my friend, is where real innovation and magic happen. Are you ready to take that journey? Let's go!

Three Insightful Questions to Ponder on This Topic

Do you encourage diverse opinions or surround yourself with echoes?

Engaging with diverse opinions is the lifeblood of innovation. As a leader or a team member, it's essential to surround oneself with a myriad of perspectives. Start by actively seeking feedback from those who might see things differently. This could be by initiating brainstorming sessions, holding regular team check-ins, or even conducting anonymous surveys. Remember, when everyone thinks the same, there's a limit to how much you can grow. Be willing to step outside your comfort zone and learn from the diverse tapestry of experiences and insights your team brings.

When faced with different views, do you get defensive or genuinely listen?

Active listening is a skill that takes practice. When someone offers a viewpoint that contrasts with your own, instead of jumping to defend your stance, take a moment to genuinely understand their perspective. By doing so, you not only validate their input but also gain insights that could enhance your own understanding. Remember, each time you choose to truly listen, you're opening doors to greater collaboration and innovation. To cultivate this skill, practice paraphrasing what the other person has said before responding, and always approach conversations with a mindset of curiosity rather than confrontation.

Have you cultivated a safe space for open discussions in your team?

Creating a psychologically safe environment is pivotal for fostering open communication and innovation. If team members fear backlash or judgment, they will hold back potentially transformative ideas. As a leader, you have the power to set the tone. Begin by encouraging open dialogue, acknowledging contributions, and addressing conflicts constructively. Most importantly, when mistakes happen, treat them as learning opportunities rather than opportunities for blame. The goal isn't to avoid mistakes but to grow from them. Celebrate the brave voices that speak up and pave the way for a culture where every idea, no matter how unconventional, is welcomed and valued.

Three Actionable Insights

Implement a "Devil's Advocate" Protocol

In meetings or brainstorming sessions, designate a "Devil's Advocate" whose role is to challenge ideas and present counterarguments. This serves multiple purposes. First, it institutionalizes the idea that dissent is not only accepted but expected. Second, it helps to depersonalize disagreements, reducing the likelihood of conflict becoming emotionally charged. The key here is to rotate this role among team members so that everyone gets comfortable with both giving and receiving constructive critique. Over time, this practice can help normalize dissent and encourage more open dialogue.

Create a Feedback Bank

Sometimes, people are uncomfortable voicing their disagreements or alternative ideas in a public setting, especially if the culture hasn't fully embraced this yet. Set up an anonymous digital "Feedback Bank" where team members can deposit their thoughts, questions, or counter-arguments. Periodically review these submissions in team meetings, giving due credit to the quality of the idea rather than the rank of the individual who submitted it. This practice serves to democratize feedback and can unearth valuable insights that might otherwise have stayed buried.

Organize Structured Debate Sessions

Go beyond regular team meetings by organizing monthly or quarterly structured debate sessions. In these sessions, teams can deep-dive into more complex issues that require thorough examination. Encourage team members to come prepared, having researched both sides of an argument. The structure can range from formal debate formats to more relaxed round-table discussions, but the aim remains the same: to rigorously test ideas and assumptions. These sessions can be invaluable in fostering a culture that not only tolerates but thrives on diverse opinions.

Personal Notes

Day 6 - Good vs Bad Leadership

"People don't leave bad jobs. They leave because of bad bosses, poor management, who don't appreciate their value."- Maya Angelou

Listen, let's cut to the chase: leadership and management aren't just buzzwords to throw around in board meetings or plaster across motivational posters. They're the lifeblood of any organization. When wielded effectively, they can turn a mediocre team into a powerhouse. Employees aren't just cogs in a machine; they're human beings craving direction, motivation, and—dare I say it—a bit of inspiration. A good leader understands this and knows how to galvanize their team, which leads to lower turnover rates and sky-high performance metrics. If your employees are sticking around and knocking it out of the park, chances are you've got someone at the helm who knows what they're doing.

On the flip side, poor leadership is an absolute disaster, a one-way ticket to a dysfunctional workplace. Ever work in an office where everyone's polishing their resumes? You can bet your bottom dollar that the leadership is rotten. When managers treat their roles as a power trip rather than a responsibility, they create a toxic environment. Employees become disengaged, morale sinks, and before you know it, your top talent is out the door, leaving you stuck in a never-ending cycle of recruitment and training. And let's not forget the hit your organizational performance takes; it's like a gut punch that keeps on giving.

Now, you might be thinking, "Well, a good leader is hard to find." True, but that's no excuse. If you're in a position of power, it's your job to either be that good leader or find someone who can fill those shoes. The cost of bad leadership is too high. We're talking about human capital here, folks—the most valuable asset in your organization. Screw that up, and you're not just losing employees; you're losing competitive advantage, customer satisfaction, and let's face it, your reputation.

And let's not overlook middle management. Often overlooked, these are the folks who are the glue between the visionary leaders and the boots-on-the-ground employees. If they're not up to snuff, you can bet that dysfunction will trickle down faster than you can say "quarterly review." Middle managers need to be effective communicators and motivators; otherwise, the best-laid plans of upper management are doomed to fail.

So, the next time you shrug off leadership and management as corporate jargon, think again. These aren't just fancy titles or cushy jobs. They're roles that come with a hell of a lot of responsibility. Good leaders motivate, inspire, and drive an organization to success. Poor leaders? Well, they're the anchor dragging everything down. And in today's cutthroat business environment, who can afford that kind of baggage?

Leadership and management are not just titles or corner offices; they're sacred trusts that you earn every single day. You're not just overseeing tasks; you're shaping lives, molding the future, and creating a culture that either fuels dreams or stifles them. Understand this: your vibe sets the tribe. When you lead with passion, empathy, and a laser focus on bringing out the best in your team, you don't just hit targets—you shatter ceilings. Your employees won't just stick around; they'll become evangelists for the incredible culture you've cultivated. That's how you build something legendary!

But hold up—let's flip the script for a second. If you're the kind of leader who thinks it's all about cracking the whip and micromanaging, you're not just damaging your team—you're sabotaging yourself. The universe has a funny way of reflecting back what you put out. So, if you're wondering why you're stuck in a revolving door of talent, take a long, hard look in the mirror. **Leadership is not about flexing your authority; it's about empowering those around you. So go ahead, unleash your inner** inspirational guru. Be the leader who doesn't just make employees stay but makes them soar. It's time to rise and shine, my friend. Your team—and the world—are waiting for your greatness.

Three Insightful Questions to Ponder on This Topic

Are you empowering your team or unknowingly limiting them?

To genuinely answer this question, you'll need to introspect deeply and perhaps even solicit feedback from your team. It can be challenging to recognize our own shortcomings, but it's crucial for growth. Start by conducting anonymous surveys where your team can share their views about your leadership style without fear of backlash. Take the time to understand the differences between transactional and transformational leadership. While the former is about tasks, rewards, and penalties, the latter is about inspiring and motivating, creating a vision, and instilling passion. By adopting more transformational leadership traits, you'll empower your team, fostering a more innovative and positive environment.

If you have middle management, do they align with your vision?

Middle management is the bridge between strategy and execution. To strengthen this bridge, invest in their training and development. Encourage them to take leadership courses and hold regular meetings with them to discuss the company's objectives and vision. Foster open communication lines, ensuring they're comfortable approaching you with challenges they face or feedback they've gathered. Moreover, build a culture where middle managers are viewed as mentors rather than just taskmasters. This will enhance their relationship with their teams, ensuring smoother execution of strategies and more cohesion throughout the organization.

Is your leadership style task-driven or people-centered?

Today's most successful organizations understand that their people are their most valuable asset. While outcomes and targets are essential, how you achieve them makes all the difference. If you're unsure about your approach, again, feedback is invaluable.

Regularly check in with your team to gauge their well-being and job satisfaction. Organize team-building activities that aren't just about work but also about bonding and understanding one another. Encourage work-life balance, as a burnt-out team won't be productive in the long run. If you find that you've been too task-focused, take steps to incorporate more empathy into your leadership. Remember, when your team feels valued and understood, they're more likely to go the extra mile for you and the organization.

Three Actionable Insights

Cultivate Emotional Agility:

You've heard of emotional intelligence, but what about emotional agility? This is the art of navigating complex emotional landscapes—both yours and your team's—with skill and grace. For instance, instead of dismissing negative emotions in the workplace, acknowledge them as signals. If your team seems stressed or disengaged, don't plaster over it with false positivity. Dig deep. Get to the root cause and address it. Emotional agility allows you to switch gears, adapting your leadership style to meet the unique needs of the situation and the individual. So, next time things get tense or awkward, instead of sidestepping, lean in. Your team will thank you for it.

Engineer Serendipity:

In a digital world, many interactions are planned down to the last detail, leaving little room for organic, off-the-cuff exchanges that can lead to innovation. Make it a point to create 'collision spaces' in your workplace—whether physical or virtual—where team members can have unplanned interactions. This could be as simple as rotating team members through different projects, setting up random "coffee chats" among employees, or using 'bump bots' in virtual settings that randomly pair team members for quick catch-ups. When you allow serendipity to take its course, you're not just fostering creativity; you're building a culture where magic can happen.

Master the Art of 'Strategic Disengagement':

This might sound counterintuitive, but sometimes the best thing a leader can do is step back. No, this isn't negligence; it's strategic disengagement. There are moments when your involvement can actually stifle your team's growth or limit their problem-solving capabilities. Recognize those moments and give your team the space to take ownership. This doesn't mean you're off the hook or aloof. You're still monitoring progress and available for guidance, but you're not micromanaging every decision. You'll be surprised how often the best solutions come when you're not breathing down someone's neck.

Personal Notes

Day 7 - Redefining Leadership Beyond Titles and Ranks

"If your actions inspire others to dream more, learn more, do more & become more, you are a leader." - John Quincy Adams

In the corridors of power, boardrooms, and academic halls, we've been sold an outdated myth: that leadership is about titles, positions, and authority. It's time to shatter that illusion. Leadership isn't a badge you wear; it's a calling you answer. It's not about where you sit in an organizational chart; it's about how you inspire those around you to rise to greatness. Leadership isn't an exclusive club for those in high-ranking positions; it's an inclusive mission that anyone can join, no matter where you stand in the hierarchy.

Think about it: Have you ever felt truly led by someone simply because they held a title? Probably not. True leadership transcends any label. It's not about being a CEO, a general, or a president.

Leadership is about inspiring others to discover their own potential. It's about motivating people to go beyond the ordinary, to tap into their best selves, and to achieve what they never thought possible. Titles may open doors, but only genuine leadership unlocks hearts.

We've been conditioned to look up—literally and figuratively—for leadership. But leadership is not a top-down concept; it's a circle that connects us all. Everyone has the power to lead because everyone has the power to inspire and motivate. Whether you're a janitor or a junior executive, your capacity for leadership isn't defined by your job description, but by your ability to lift others up.

In this shift in understanding, we liberate leadership from the shackles of tradition and exclusivity. We make it accessible, achievable, and authentically human. We free it from the restraints of social status and rank, and we anchor it in the qualities that matter most: inspiration, motivation, and interpersonal connection. Leadership becomes not just a role to aspire to, but a quality to embody—right here, right now.

Listen up, because I've got something game-changing to tell you: Leadership is not a title, it's not a position, and it sure isn't a corner office. Forget the old-school playbook that tells you leadership is about rank and authority. That's yesterday's news! You don't need a fancy title to be a leader; you just need the courage to inspire and uplift those around you. Leadership is a vibe, an energy, a transformative force that flows from you to everyone you touch. It's about making people believe in themselves, so much so that they go beyond their limitations and do things they never thought possible. Whether you're a cashier, a teacher, or a stay-at-home parent, know this: You have the power to lead, right where you are.

So, let's redefine this thing called leadership, shall we? Let's make it something that each and every one of us can embody. Stop waiting for someone to give you permission to lead. You don't need permission; you've got purpose! Leadership isn't about sitting at the top;

it's about lifting others up. You have that fire within you—ignite it, let it blaze, and light up the world around you. **From this moment on, don't just aim to be someone in charge; strive to be someone who changes lives. Because when you lead with your heart, titles become irrelevant and impact becomes inevitable. Let's go out there and lead like we mean it!**

Three Insightful Questions to Ponder on This Topic

Do you see leadership as a title or an inherent quality?

It's easy to fall into the trap of associating leadership with external symbols of authority. But true leadership is an internal quality. Begin by introspecting on your past experiences. Think of times when you were inspired or motivated by someone who wasn't necessarily in a "leader" position. Use those memories as a reminder that true leadership is about influence, not authority. To cultivate this perspective further, focus on developing your interpersonal skills, empathetic listening, and your ability to inspire and motivate. Remember, every interaction is an opportunity to lead.

How do you inspire others, regardless of your position?

Leadership opportunities are everywhere, often in places we least expect them. Start by assessing your current role and identifying areas where you can make a positive impact. It could be as simple as mentoring a colleague, recognizing and praising someone's hard work, or offering a fresh perspective in a team meeting. The key is to be proactive, not reactive. Instead of waiting for leadership moments to come to you, create them. And remember, leadership isn't about imposing your will on others; it's about guiding, supporting, and empowering.

Are societal norms or self-doubt holding back your leadership potential?

Many of us hold back because of internalized beliefs about what we can or cannot achieve, often influenced by societal definitions or past experiences. Start by challenging these beliefs. Write them down and question their validity. For every limiting belief, find a counter example or argument. Engage in self-development activities, read books on leadership and personal growth, or consider finding a mentor. The more you invest in your personal growth, the more you'll realize that you're capable of much more than you previously thought. As you grow, your ability to lead will naturally expand, regardless of external titles or societal expectations.

Three Actionable Insights

Practice "Reverse Mentoring":

In a traditional mentoring setup, the senior person mentors the junior person. Flip that script! Invite a junior team member to share their insights and skills with you or the team. Whether it's a fresh perspective on technology or a new market trend, this exchange not only fosters a sense of inclusivity but also signals that leadership is about continuous learning from all directions. You demonstrate that titles are irrelevant when it comes to gaining wisdom, and everyone has something valuable to offer.

Introduce "Idea Amnesty":

Create a safe space or a particular time where any team member can bring up an idea without fear of judgment or immediate critique. Call it an "Idea Amnesty Hour." The focus is not on the feasibility of the idea but on the courage to share it. When you celebrate the act of idea-sharing, you encourage even the quietest voices to speak up. This practice proves that leadership doesn't rest with those who hold the power to implement ideas but also with those who dare to dream them up in the first place.

Initiate "Random Acts of Leadership":
Don't wait for quarterly reviews or team meetings to showcase leadership. Turn everyday actions into leadership moments. Help a colleague with a task unsolicited, offer constructive feedback when not expected, or even share a relevant article that could benefit your peers. These random acts of leadership show that you don't need a planned agenda or a captive audience to lead. You're taking the initiative to positively influence your environment, one small act at a time.

Personal Notes

Day 8 - The Power of Trust in Leadership

"When we tell people to do their jobs, we get workers. When we trust people to get the job done, we get leaders."- Simon Sinek

Trust is an indispensable element in the fabric of effective leadership and organizational success. It serves as the cornerstone upon which teams build their capacity for collaborative problem-solving, innovation, and risk-taking. In a high-trust environment, team members feel secure in expressing their ideas without the fear of ridicule or judgment, which in turn fosters open communication. This level of freedom ignites creativity and encourages individuals to explore unconventional approaches, often leading to groundbreaking solutions. Moreover, the willingness to take calculated risks—crucial for any organization aiming to stay competitive in today's rapidly evolving markets—is significantly enhanced when team members trust that their leaders and colleagues will support them, irrespective of the outcome.

Trust is not just a feel-good factor; it translates into quantifiable business advantages. Organizations with high levels of trust consistently outperform those that lack this crucial element, both in terms of productivity and employee engagement. Team members in a high-trust setting are more committed, display greater loyalty, and are more likely to go the extra mile, all of which contribute to an efficient and successful workplace. Additionally, high-trust organizations experience lower turnover rates, which is significant given that the recruitment and training of new employees can be both time-consuming and costly.

While trust is beneficial at every level of an organization, its cultivation is chiefly the responsibility of its leaders. Trust is often built through consistency, openness, and a genuine concern for the welfare of team members. Leaders must act as role models, demonstrating integrity and transparency in their actions. They should also encourage an open culture where employees feel comfortable sharing their thoughts and concerns. A leader's ability to show vulnerability, admit mistakes, and treat failures as learning opportunities can go a long way in establishing a high-trust environment.

In the context of modern organizations, which are increasingly characterized by complex projects, cross-functional teams, and a need for rapid decision-making, trust is more vital than ever. The days of top-down, command-and-control leadership are long gone. Today's leaders are facilitators who enable their teams to achieve their best work. In such a scenario, the absence of trust can lead to a breakdown in communication, a reluctance to share information, and ultimately, project failure.

Listen, if you're in a leadership role or aspiring to be one, you've got to understand that trust is your secret weapon. It's the magic ingredient that can transform your team from a group of individuals into a powerhouse of creativity and innovation. Imagine a team where everyone feels safe to speak their mind, share their craziest ideas, and take risks—because they know they're supported and valued. That's what trust does! It liberates people to give their absolute best, to go the extra mile, and to innovate like they've never done before. And guess what? This all starts with you—the leader. You've got the power to create this culture of trust, so wield it wisely and generously.

Now, building trust isn't just about what you say; it's about what you do, day in and day out. Be the leader who shows up, who listens, and who leads with integrity and openness. When you make a mistake—and we all do—own it and treat it as a learning opportunity for everyone. You see, people don't just follow titles; they follow courage. They follow authenticity. **So, be the leader who lays the foundation of trust, and watch how it revolutionizes your team's dynamics, boosts morale, and catapults your organizational success to heights you never thought possible. You've got this!**

Three Insightful Questions to Ponder on This Topic

Is your work environment open for candid discussions?

Building a safe environment isn't just about avoiding criticism; it's about creating a culture where feedback, both positive and constructive, is welcomed and appreciated. Leaders should facilitate open dialogues, where team members feel their opinions are valued and considered. Encourage brainstorming sessions, and make it a point to recognize and appreciate new ideas. When concerns are raised, address them promptly and ensure that the team member feels heard. A practical way to measure this is to ask for feedback anonymously about the openness of team discussions and act on suggestions given.

Are you authentic and consistent, especially during tough times?

Consistency is key in leadership. Team members find comfort in knowing what to expect, and unpredictable behavior can erode trust rapidly. Leading with authenticity means being true to yourself, admitting when you don't know something, and being transparent about decisions. During challenging times, rather than hiding or downplaying issues, communicate openly with your team. Share the problem, invite solutions, and make collaborative decisions. Remember, authenticity also means admitting mistakes. When you own up to an error, it not only shows humility but also sets a standard for the team about the importance of learning from mistakes rather than fearing them.

How do you handle vulnerability and failures?

Vulnerability is not about weakness; it's about showing your human side. It's about admitting when you're unsure, seeking help, and sharing personal experiences that shaped your leadership journey. By showcasing vulnerability, you make yourself more relatable and approachable. When it comes to failures, instead of laying blame, treat them as learning opportunities. Organize 'retrospective' or 'post-mortem' meetings after projects to discuss what went well and what could be improved, ensuring the focus is on the process and not on individuals. Celebrate the effort and the learnings that come from failures. This approach not only fosters resilience but also encourages team members to take calculated risks, knowing that even if they don't succeed, they'll learn and grow.

Three Actionable Insights

Implement "Trust Audits":

Conduct periodic "Trust Audits" to gauge the level of trust within your team or organization. Use anonymous surveys or facilitated group discussions to assess how team members feel about the trustworthiness of leadership and their colleagues. Ask questions that explore the integrity, reliability, and openness of individuals within the team. Use this feedback to identify areas for improvement and to develop specific action plans. Remember, trust is not static; it needs continuous attention and re-evaluation.

Establish a "Failure Forum":

Create a regular meeting space called the "Failure Forum" where team members can openly discuss mistakes or setbacks they've experienced. The objective isn't to chastise but to extract valuable lessons and to normalize the idea that failures are a part of the learning process. This will help team members feel more comfortable with taking risks, as they understand that even if things don't go as planned, the focus will be on learning and growing rather than assigning blame.

Initiate "Silent Meetings":

Silent meetings can be incredibly effective in ensuring that everyone's voice is heard, thereby building trust. In these meetings, rather than speaking, participants write down their thoughts and ideas on a shared document. After a set period, everyone reviews the document and discussions commence. This practice ensures that those who are typically less vocal have an equal opportunity to contribute. It also minimizes the impact of dominant personalities, allowing for more equitable participation and fostering a sense of trust that everyone's input is valued.

Personal Notes

Day 9 - Choosing the Right Circle of Influence

"Surround yourself with people that push you to do and be better. No drama or negativity. Just higher goals and higher motivation. Good times and positive energy. No jealousy or hate. Simply bringing out the absolute best in each other."- Warren Buffet

In a world that constantly pushes us to evolve, the people you surround yourself with aren't just company—they're catalysts for your success or mediocrity. Even more so in unprecedented times, when the seas are rough and the winds are turbulent, the crew you have on your life's ship determines if you'll merely survive or truly thrive. Now, more than ever, is the time to be judicious in choosing who you allow into your inner circle. The stakes are not just high; they're exponential.

You see, our destinies are not just shaped by our actions, but also by our associations. Surround yourself with positive, ambitious individuals and you'll find that their radiant energy ignites your path, lighting up opportunities you might have missed in the darkness of negativity. These are the people who not only dream but also inspire you to set the bar higher, challenging your limits. In challenging times, these are the voices that tell you, "You can," when the world screams, "You can't."

On the flip side, associating with negative or self-destructive people is akin to attaching a metaphorical anchor to your aspirations. They will pull you down faster than you can swim up, drowning your dreams in an ocean of pessimism and lost opportunities. Especially when the going gets tough, these are the individuals who will infect you with their fears, cloud your judgment, and derail your focus. The advice is simple but crucial: disassociate before you disintegrate.

Now, you might wonder, how do you make this all-important choice? Listen to your intuition and observe. Are the people around you problem solvers or problem creators? Do they elevate your thinking, or do they drag it into the abyss of their limitations? Your internal compass knows more than you give it credit for; let it guide you toward a circle that enriches, rather than diminishes, you.

Listen up, because this could be the game-changer you've been waiting for! You are the CEO of your own life, and guess what? You get to pick your board of directors—those key individuals who influence your thoughts, emotions, and actions. Don't underestimate this power, especially when the world around you seems like a rollercoaster of uncertainties. This is the moment to surround yourself with people who not only believe in your dreams but also make you believe you can achieve them. You need people who look adversity in the eye and say, "Is that all you got?" Because when you're fighting the good fight, you want warriors, not worriers, by your side!

So, make the choice NOW! Audit your circle. Who's lifting you up, and who's pulling you down? Life is too short and the climb too steep to carry dead weight. Uncertainty can either paralyze you or galvanize you into action. Let's make sure it's the latter, and let's make sure you've got a team around you that's charging up that mountain alongside you, cheering you on every step of the way! **You've got this, but you don't have to do it alone. So go ahead, build your dream team and let's turn those dreams into reality!**

Three Insightful Questions to Ponder on This Topic

Are negative influences affecting your decisions?

Take a moment to reflect on the interactions you have on a daily basis. If you notice a recurring pattern of negativity or a consistent drain on your energy after spending time with certain individuals, it might be an indication that their influence is holding you back. Progress requires a positive and growth-oriented environment. If certain relationships seem to consistently drain your energy, consider setting boundaries or limiting your interactions with these individuals. Remember, it's essential for your growth to surround yourself with those who encourage your ambitions, not hinder them.

Does your inner circle elevate or limit you?

Growth often comes from discomfort and being pushed beyond what we perceive as our limits. Your inner circle should consist of individuals who can constructively challenge you and help you see the potential within yourself. If you find that your closest relationships predominantly feed your fears or doubt your capabilities, it might be time to expand your circle. Attend networking events, join clubs or organizations related to your interests, or engage in community service. These activities can introduce you to positive, like-minded individuals who can support and uplift you.

Have you chosen the right influencers in your life?

It's easy to fall into the comfort of routine and familiarity. However, as the CEO of your life, it's crucial to actively select who gets a seat at your table. Regularly audit your relationships. Reflect on the value each person brings to your life, not in a transactional sense, but in terms of emotional, intellectual, and spiritual growth. If someone is consistently detracting from your well-being or growth, it might be time to reevaluate their place in your inner circle. Remember, it's not about cutting people out in a cold or callous manner but ensuring that you're curating a circle that aligns with your life's vision and goals. Your time and energy are valuable, so invest them in relationships that nurture and propel you forward.

Three Actionable Insights

Implement a "Vibe Check" System:

In the hustle and bustle of the workplace, it's easy to overlook the emotional climate that pervades your team or department. Introduce a "Vibe Check" system where team members briefly share their state of mind or emotional 'temperature' at the beginning of meetings. It's not about diving into personal issues, but rather a quick way to gauge the collective energy. This practice will make it apparent who consistently brings a constructive, positive vibe that contributes to productivity and who does not. Over time, this will help you decide which colleagues you should gravitate towards for collaborative efforts.

Initiate "Elevator Pitch Mondays":

Start your week with a quick team session where each member gives an 'elevator pitch' on what they aim to accomplish that week and how it aligns with the team's or company's goals. This is a two-fold strategy. First, it helps identify the go-getters and ambitious thinkers in your circle, those you might want to align yourself with. Second, it serves as a motivational tool, creating a sense of accountability. When everyone starts their week setting high standards, it elevates the entire team's performance.

Develop a "Growth Partner" System:

Pair up team members as "Growth Partners" for a defined period, say a month or a quarter. The role of a Growth Partner is to act as a mini-mentor and accountability buddy. They check in with each other regularly to discuss challenges, share constructive feedback, and celebrate wins, big or small. This exercise can be particularly eye-opening. It lets you experience firsthand the impact of close association with different kinds of individuals and helps you make informed decisions about who you should be spending more time with professionally

Personal Notes

Day 10 - Why Employee Turnover is Your Wake-Up Call

"Management is doing things right; leadership is doing the right things." - Peter Drucker.

Listen up, leaders. You're at the wheel of this ship, and if people are jumping overboard, it's high time to question your navigation skills, not blame the waters. Let's be real; when an employee walks out the door, it's not always about a bigger paycheck or a shorter commute. More often than not, they're running away from poor leadership. "People don't leave jobs; they leave bosses," goes the saying. Ever heard of it? You should, because it's your wake-up call.

You might think you're doing a stellar job, but if your team's turnover rate skyrockets, you're missing the mark. It's a glaring red flag, and don't delude yourself into thinking it's just a fluke or a 'them issue.' A revolving door of employees costs you not just in recruitment and training, but it erodes the very fabric of your organization—morale. Imagine being part of a team where the MVPs are always calling it quits. Demoralizing, isn't it? Now, what does that say about your leadership?

Now, I'm not saying you're the villain here, but if the shoe fits—introspection is the first step toward change. Ever paused to think why that star employee really left? Was it your lack of communication or, perhaps, your failure to recognize their efforts? It's easy to brush it off and say, "Oh, they weren't a good fit." But what if the problem is that your leadership style isn't a 'good fit' for anyone who values respect and growth? The exit of an employee is a glaring mirror reflecting on your management style. Are you brave enough to look into it?

Alright, you get it; there's a problem. But griping about it won't fix it. You need to act, and act fast. Open those lines of communication. Be the kind of leader who cultivates an environment where feedback—yes, even the uncomfortable, critical kind—is welcomed. Address issues head-on instead of sweeping them under the rug. And for heaven's sake, when someone resigns, take it as constructive criticism. Dig deep, find the root cause, and course-correct before you're steering a ghost ship.

I know leading a team isn't a walk in the park, but guess what? You've got an incredible opportunity every single day to make a lasting impact on people's lives. Yeah, you heard me right. People may walk into your office because of the job, but they'll stay—or leave—because of you. When someone hands in their resignation, it's not a failure; it's a feedback form in disguise. A golden ticket for you to get even better at what you do. So don't dwell on the negative; seize that moment as your chance to grow, to learn, and to become the kind of leader people would follow to the ends of the earth!

So, the next time someone leaves, don't just ask yourself why they left; ask yourself why the others are staying. Then multiply that goodness! Open your door, lend an ear, and let your team know that their opinions matter. Because a great leader doesn't just have followers; a great leader creates an environment where everyone feels like they're part of something bigger than themselves. This is your arena, your moment. Own it! **Let those resignations be the stepping stones on your path to becoming an extraordinary leader. You've got the power to turn things around, so what are you waiting for? Go out there and show the world what you're made of!**

Three Insightful Questions to Ponder on This Topic

Do you understand your team's concerns and feelings?

Self-awareness is a key aspect of effective leadership. Even if you believe you're doing everything right, there might be underlying issues you're unaware of. Consider conducting anonymous surveys within your team to gather feedback on your leadership style, communication effectiveness, and overall work environment. By doing this, you can get an unfiltered view of areas you excel in and those you need to improve. Additionally, consider seeking a mentor or coach who can give you constructive feedback and help you see things from a different perspective.

Is your team comfortable sharing their thoughts with you?

Psychological safety is crucial for an environment where team members feel comfortable speaking up. If people are hesitant to voice their concerns or share ideas, it's possible they fear retribution or feel their opinions aren't valued. Start by setting the example—demonstrate that you value feedback by actively seeking it and responding positively when you receive it. Encourage open communication in meetings and one-on-one sessions. Show that every opinion is valuable, and there's no penalty for constructive dissent. Over time, this will cultivate trust and a more collaborative environment.

When did you last celebrate your team's achievements?

Recognition can go a long way in boosting morale and reinforcing positive behavior. People want to know their hard work is seen and valued. It doesn't always require grand gestures; simple acts, like sending a thank-you note or publicly acknowledging someone's contribution in a team meeting, can make a significant difference. Set aside regular intervals, perhaps monthly or quarterly, to celebrate team and individual achievements. This not only boosts morale but also fosters a sense of community and team spirit.

Remember, employees who feel recognized and appreciated are more likely to go the extra mile and less likely to seek opportunities elsewhere.

Three Actionable Insights

Deploy a "Skip-Level Meeting" Strategy:

Skip-level meetings involve leaders meeting with employees who are one or more levels below them in the organizational hierarchy, skipping the immediate manager.

Schedule regular skip-level meetings, say once a quarter, where you talk to team members two or more tiers below you. Make sure these meetings are confidential and intended for genuine conversations about the work environment, challenges, and opportunities for innovation.

It provides you with unfiltered insights about your team and management layers, directly from the people who are affected by it. This information can be gold when you're trying to understand why employees might be leaving.

Launch a "Peer Review 360" Program:

Unlike traditional reviews where only managers provide feedback, a Peer Review 360 involves team members reviewing each other, as well as themselves.

Initiate a semi-annual or annual Peer Review 360 program. Make it anonymous to encourage candid feedback. Use this data to identify patterns or areas where management—including you—can improve.

This kind of all-around feedback helps you to see blind spots in your leadership style that you might not be aware of. More importantly, it makes everyone accountable for the team's culture and performance, not just the leader.

Implement a "Job Rotation" Scheme:

Job Rotation involves moving team members through a variety of roles within the organization, temporarily changing their responsibilities.

Every six months, give team members the option to switch roles with someone else in the team or even in a different department. Ensure that each switch involves a brief training period for the new role and set expectations clearly.

Job rotation helps you identify hidden talents and skills within your team. It also allows team members to understand the challenges and responsibilities their peers face, fostering empathy. This broadened perspective often leads to improved teamwork and reveals any systemic issues that could be causing employee dissatisfaction.

Personal Notes

Day 11 - Conquer Challenges and Step Out of Your Comfort Zone

"Comfort is your biggest trap and coming out of comfort zone your biggest challenge." - Manoj Arora

When it comes to being a good leader, just being talented or skilled isn't enough. What sets true leaders apart is their indomitable spirit—a willingness to face challenges head-on, confront their fears, and navigate through obstacles. Leadership demands more than a theoretical understanding of what should be done; it calls for a visceral commitment to doing what must be done, even when it involves stepping into the unknown. Venturing out of one's comfort zone is not a mere luxury; it is a prerequisite for the transformative growth that leadership entails.

The essence of leadership lies in the potent blend of vision and action. While the former gives direction, it is the latter—action—that carves out a path through the wilderness of challenges. An effective leader does not merely envisage an end; they continually adapt and muster the courage to achieve it. This often involves confronting fears that act as psychological barriers—fears of failure, judgment, or even the unknown. Overcoming these fears is not an act of bravery but a calculated choice that underscores the leader's commitment to their cause.

Moreover, obstacles are not to be viewed as roadblocks but as stepping stones on the path to success. When faced with challenges, the leader's role is to dissect them analytically, understand their root causes, and formulate strategies to surmount them. In doing so, the leader is not just solving problems but also setting a precedent for their team. The leader cultivates a culture where challenges are viewed as opportunities for growth and innovation, thus fostering a resilient and adaptive organization.

However, it is crucial to recognize that leadership is not a solitary endeavor. The leader must not only be willing to explore new opportunities but also be adept at inspiring their team to do the same. This involves cultivating an environment where each member is encouraged to push their boundaries and explore new avenues for growth. By stepping out of the comfort zone, not only does the leader grow, but they also facilitate an environment that nurtures the holistic development of their team.

You know, life is packed full of challenges and roadblocks, but guess what? That's your training ground! Those fears you're feeling, those obstacles getting in your way—they're not stopping you; they're making you. Each challenge is a question asking, "How badly do you want it?" Don't shy away; step up! Confront your fears, tackle those obstacles, and turn them into stepping stones. Remember, a smooth sea never made a skilled sailor. You've got to sail through those storms to find your true north.

Now, let's talk about that comfort zone—it's cozy, it's familiar, but it's also where dreams go to die. If you want to be a game-changing leader, you've got to step out and stretch those boundaries. Yeah, it's scary, but that's where the magic happens. You grow, your team grows, and together, you create something extraordinary. So, what are you waiting for? **The world doesn't need more people playing it safe; the world needs bold, courageous leaders willing to face challenges head-on. Be that leader. Transform not just your life, but the lives of those around you. Go out there and own it!**

Three Insightful Questions to Ponder on This Topic

Do you venture beyond your comfort zone or stay within it?

If you find yourself frequently retreating to familiar territory, remember that real growth happens at the edges of discomfort. This doesn't mean you should actively seek discomfort for its own sake, but instead, recognize the opportunities embedded within challenges. Start small. Set one achievable goal that's just slightly outside your comfort zone and work towards it. Celebrate your successes along the way, no matter how minor they seem. By incrementally pushing your boundaries, you'll expand your comfort zone over time and become more adaptable and resilient in the face of adversity.

Are obstacles setbacks or growth opportunities for you?

It's natural to initially perceive obstacles as setbacks, but transformative leaders recognize the value in reframing challenges as opportunities. Instead of avoiding them, delve into understanding the root cause of these obstacles. By adopting a problem-solving mindset, you not only overcome the immediate hurdle but also equip yourself with the knowledge and skills to tackle similar challenges in the future. Encourage your team to adopt this perspective as well, fostering a culture where challenges are met with curiosity, creativity, and collaboration.

Are you promoting innovation or caution in your team?

Leading by example is the most potent tool at your disposal. If you showcase a willingness to venture into the unknown, take risks, and consistently push your limits, your team will feel more empowered to do the same. Regularly engage in open dialogues with your team, creating a safe space where they can share their ideas, fears, and aspirations. Celebrate their achievements, especially when they've pushed past their comfort zones. Implement feedback loops to understand if there are any systemic barriers or fears holding them back. Remember, the objective is not just personal growth but creating an environment where every team member feels motivated to reach their highest potential.

Three Actionable Insights

Execute "Challenge Swaps":

The concept is simple but effective: team members briefly exchange tasks that are outside of their usual responsibilities but aligned with their professional growth. For instance, if one team member is great at data analysis but poor at public speaking, and another excels in client relations but struggles with project management, have them swap a task for a week. This forces individuals to confront challenges and fears they might otherwise avoid, providing a safe yet impactful learning experience.

Adopt a "Two-Week Experiment" Framework:

Innovation often stagnates because of the fear of long-term consequences. What if you could minimize this risk? Introduce a culture where team members can propose and run experiments designed to improve workflows, generate more sales, or enhance product quality. However, the experiment should be time-bound, lasting no more than two weeks. This minimizes the fear associated with failure and facilitates a faster feedback loop. At the end of two weeks, assess the results together and decide whether the new approach should be integrated, modified, or discarded.

Implement a "Courage Award":

We often reward success but overlook the courage it takes to attempt something new. Create a monthly or quarterly "Courage Award" for the individual or team who took on the most challenging project or task, irrespective of the outcome. The key criteria for the award should be the level of challenge involved and the learning acquired during the process, not just the end result. This will encourage people to step out of their comfort zones and tackle more complex issues, as they know their efforts will be acknowledged.

Personal Notes

Day 12 - Positive Leadership: A Catalyst for Success

"Leaders are responsible for creating an environment where people can be at their best." – Simon Sinek

The role of leadership in shaping an organization's environment cannot be overstated. Great leaders have the ability to transform an ordinary setting into a fertile ground for innovation, collaboration, and success. One of the most significant ways they achieve this is by making their employees feel safe and empowered. In a work culture nurtured by positive leadership, employees are encouraged to take risks without the fear of reprisal, ask questions to foster growth, and make decisions that align with organizational objectives. This sense of psychological safety enables them to stretch their capabilities and become the best versions of themselves.

On the flip side, poor leadership can serve as a corrosive element in any organization. Leaders who are dictatorial, unapproachable, or dismissive create an atmosphere of tension and anxiety. In such toxic environments, the focus of employees shifts from innovation and cooperation to mere self-preservation. Employees become risk-averse, as making a mistake can often lead to punitive measures. Consequently, they stop contributing meaningfully to the organization and instead focus on just "getting by." The ripple effect of this survivalist attitude can significantly damage an organization's long-term prospects.

The style of leadership not only affects the well-being of the employees but also the overall health of the organization. An empowering leader acts as a unifying force, fostering a culture of openness, respect, and shared objectives. This sense of unity and purpose equips the organization with an invisible armor against external threats and challenges. In contrast, a toxic leader can splinter the workforce, eroding the organization's internal stability and resilience. When faced with external pressures, such an organization is likely to crumble as its foundational culture is already weakened.

Employee well-being is not a peripheral issue; it is central to the success or failure of an organization. The emotional and psychological state of the workforce is a direct reflection of the leadership style. Employees who feel valued, respected, and empowered are likely to be more engaged, motivated, and committed to their roles. They not only contribute to a positive work environment but also become ambassadors for the organizational brand. In contrast, employees suffering under toxic leadership are likely to be disengaged, demotivated, and potentially seeking opportunities elsewhere, which further perpetuates a cycle of underperformance.

Listen, you have an incredible power within you—the power to lead, to inspire, and to change lives. Whether you're leading a team, a department, or an entire organization, remember that your style of leadership doesn't just impact the bottom line, it touches lives. Great leaders create more than just successful projects; they build a sanctuary where people's spirits can flourish. When your team feels safe, valued, and empowered, they won't just meet targets, they'll exceed them. They'll bring their A-game every single day, not because they have to, but because they WANT to. So, be that beacon of positive energy, be that catalyst for change!

Now, let's talk about the flip side. Toxic leadership doesn't just hurt your team; it chips away at the soul of your organization. When people are more concerned about surviving the workday than contributing to the mission, you've already lost the game. Don't be the leader who plants seeds of doubt and fear. Be the leader who cultivates confidence, growth, and opportunity. **Your leadership style is a legacy that you leave behind at every interaction, every meeting, and every decision. Make it a legacy that uplifts everyone around you, fortifying your organization against challenges and setting the stage for success that endures. You've got this! Now go out there and make a difference!**

Three Insightful Questions to Ponder on This Topic

Do team members feel safe to share ideas with you?

To ensure you're fostering a sense of psychological safety, begin by opening up regular channels of communication with your team. This might be through weekly check-ins, anonymous suggestion boxes, or open-door policies. When a team member approaches with an idea or concern, actively listen without interruption, and thank them for their contribution. Avoid immediate judgment or dismissal. Over time, as you consistently show that you value their input and that there won't be negative repercussions for speaking up, you'll find more team members actively participating and contributing to the organization's goals. Furthermore, consider providing training or workshops that focus on constructive feedback, ensuring that even if the feedback is critical, it's delivered in a way that fosters growth and not fear.

How do you ensure your leadership is uplifting, not oppressive?

Self-awareness is the first step towards empowering leadership. Set aside time for introspection and assess your interactions with your team. Actively seek out feedback—consider utilizing 360-degree feedback tools that allow subordinates, peers, and superiors to provide input on your leadership style. Understand that no leader is perfect; everyone has areas for improvement. Once you identify areas where your leadership may lean towards being 'toxic,' actively work to rectify those behaviors. Engage in leadership training or coaching if necessary. Remember, it's essential to not just be a leader in title but to lead by example, demonstrating the values and behaviors you wish to see in your organization.

Are employees satisfied or leaving frequently?

High turnover rates and a pervasive sense of dissatisfaction among employees can often be symptoms of deeper organizational issues, many of which stem from leadership styles. To cultivate a positive environment, start by recognizing and rewarding the efforts and achievements of your employees. Celebrate team successes, and when there are failures, approach them as learning opportunities rather than assigning blame. Encourage team bonding through retreats, workshops, or even simple team lunches. Regularly check in with your employees to understand their career goals and aspirations and see how you, as a leader, can facilitate their growth. Investing in the personal and professional growth of your employees not only benefits them but the organization as a whole, leading to a more committed and motivated workforce.

Three Actionable Insights

Initiate "Walk-and-Talk" Sessions:

With work moving at a mile a minute these days, it's so easy to get stuck in back-to-back meetings and endless phone calls. But when was the last time you took a moment to really connect with your team outside the office walls? Initiate "Walk-and-Talk" sessions, where instead of sitting across a desk, you and your team members go for a walk. This simple change in environment can significantly shift the dynamics of the conversation, making it less formal and more candid. The physical movement promotes better thinking and the casual setting often encourages more open dialogue. Plus, it's a great way to show your team you care about their well-being, both physically and emotionally.

Implement "Skill Shares":

Everyone in your team has unique skills and experiences that are not necessarily part of their job descriptions. Create a monthly "Skill Share" session where team members can teach others something new. This could be anything from coding tricks, public speaking tips, to even making the best cup of coffee! This is not just about adding another skill to one's repertoire; it's about recognizing and valuing the diversity of talents within your team. It fosters a culture of mutual respect and amplifies the notion that everyone has something valuable to offer.

Launch "Gratitude Fridays":
Amid the hustle and bustle of deadlines and targets, it's easy to forget the small wins and the people who make them possible. Introduce a "Gratitude Friday" ritual, where at the end of the week, team members share something they are thankful for. This could be an accomplishment, a lesson learned, or simply expressing gratitude towards a team member for their help or positive attitude. This simple act of reflection and appreciation fosters a positive work environment and reminds everyone that they are a valued part of the team. Over time, you'll find that this small investment of time has a compounding effect on team morale and overall happiness.

Personal Notes

Day 13 - Turn Your Business into a Thriving Family

"There's no magic formula for great company culture. The key is just to treat your staff how you would like to be treated." – Richard Branson

What is it that sets a thriving business apart from the rest? Why do some companies seem to effortlessly attract top talent, foster innovation, and continuously excel in their industries? The answer, my friends, is not as elusive as you might think; it boils down to the power of company culture. A strong, distinct culture isn't just a perk—it's the lifeblood of a successful organization. It transforms a workplace into more than just a space where tasks are completed; it becomes a living, breathing entity, fuelled by a shared set of values and a sense of family.

Now, let's dig into this a bit more. Why would a "family spirit" be of any relevance in a business setting? For starters, when employees feel like they belong, they are intrinsically motivated to go above and beyond. In a family, you don't merely do things because you're aiming for some financial gain; you do them because you care about the well-being of the unit as a whole. Similarly, in a company with a strong culture, employees are motivated by a collective ambition, a mutual drive for excellence. This emotional investment is the secret sauce that leads to increased productivity, innovation, and yes, profitability.

But don't just take my word for it; the numbers speak for themselves. Companies that invest in their culture report higher levels of employee engagement, lower turnover, and superior financial performance compared to their peers. So, if you're still skeptical, I challenge you to look at the data. Better yet, talk to the employees. You'll find that they're not just working for a paycheck; they're working towards a shared vision that makes every challenge surmountable and every success sweeter.

Consider your company culture as the DNA of your organization. It's the unique identifier that sets you apart from the competition. Just as DNA consists of various elements that work in harmony, so should your culture. It should be a balanced blend of values, practices, and shared aspirations. When executed well, this intricate tapestry of factors leads to a work environment that not only attracts the best and brightest but also keeps them engaged and driven— ultimately propelling the company toward greater heights.

Let's talk about something that's more than just a buzzword—it's the secret sauce to success, and it's called company culture. Imagine walking into work every day and feeling like you're part of something bigger, a place where everyone is driven by a shared vision, not just a paycheck. This is where the magic happens, my friends! A strong, united culture is like a family, and just like in any loving family, you'll find support, encouragement, and a collective will to conquer any challenge. Trust me, when you build a culture like this, you're not just clocking in and out;

you're making history, you're setting records, you're going places!

So, are you ready to be a game-changer? Stop settling for mediocrity! You have the power to create an environment that's not only fulfilling but also wildly successful. Start with small steps—open dialogues, team collaborations, and shared goals. And if you're skeptical, just look at the giants in any industry; their success isn't a fluke, it's built on a rock-solid culture. So go ahead, invest in building that invincible culture. **Make your company a family that everyone wants to be a part of, and watch how you not only attract the best talent but also achieve successes you've only dreamed of. The time is now; ignite that spark and let's set the world on fire!**

Three Insightful Questions to Ponder on This Topic

Does your company culture match its vision and values?

Start by auditing your current company culture. Begin with open-ended conversations with team members at all levels—this will give you an authentic feel for the prevailing attitudes, beliefs, and practices. Survey tools can also be used for more structured feedback. Once you have a clearer picture, compare this with the company's stated values and goals. If there's a misalignment, it's crucial to address this discrepancy. Remember, a strong culture isn't just about having values but truly living by them. To align culture with vision and values, consider hosting collaborative workshops, providing continuous training, and leading by example. The more the leadership exemplifies the desired culture, the easier it becomes for employees to emulate and adapt.

How are you promoting unity and shared vision in your team?

Fostering a family spirit starts with trust, transparency, and open communication. Regularly hold team-building activities that focus not just on work but also on getting to know each other on a personal level. Celebrate milestones, both professional and personal, and encourage collaboration and mentorship within the team. Creating spaces where employees can share their ideas and concerns without judgment is vital. Remember, in a family, every member has a voice, and their opinions are valued. Moreover, investing in continuous feedback and recognition systems can empower employees to voice concerns and feel valued for their contributions. Lastly, always prioritize the well-being of your employees; when they know that their welfare is important to the company, they'll naturally reciprocate with loyalty and dedication.

What's your next move to improve company culture?

Start by setting a clear vision for your desired culture. This should be collaborative—get input from various departments and levels within your company. Once you have that vision, communicate it clearly and consistently. Secondly, encourage open dialogue. Allow employees to share their thoughts, feedback, and suggestions regarding the current culture and ways to improve it. Consider implementing regular "culture check-ins" in team meetings. Thirdly, lead by example. If you want a culture of punctuality, be punctual. If you seek a culture of innovation, be the first to applaud new ideas and take calculated risks. Additionally, invest in training and development. When employees see a pathway for growth and continuous learning within the company, they'll feel more connected and invested. Lastly, celebrate successes, no matter how small, and always take them as opportunities to reinforce the desired culture. Remember, culture building is an ongoing process; consistency is key.

Three Actionable Insights

Host "Life Swap" Days:

The concept behind "Life Swap" Days is to give team members a deeper insight into the lives of their colleagues. Once a month, let employees pair up and swap roles for a day. This doesn't just mean job functions but also includes attending each other's meetings, and engaging with each other's daily challenges. The goal here is twofold: to cultivate empathy by walking a mile in someone else's shoes, and to encourage cross-departmental understanding. When people understand the roles, struggles, and contributions of their colleagues, it fosters a sense of unity and family spirit.

Initiate "Quarterly Culture Quests":

Take team building to the next level with "Quarterly Culture Quests." These are more than just team outings; they're adventures or challenges that are aligned with the company's core values. For example, if one of your values is sustainability, the quest could be a community cleanup. If innovation is a key value, the quest might be a hackathon. The quests serve as a living, breathing representation of what your company stands for, making the culture palpable and the values actionable. Plus, the shared experiences and stories from these quests can become part of the company folklore, strengthening the family vibe.

Establish "Personal Milestone Celebrations":
In most companies, professional milestones like work anniversaries or completed projects are celebrated, but what about personal milestones? Things like running a marathon, buying a house, or even accomplishing a personal goal are monumental for individuals. Create a platform or a monthly meeting where employees can share and celebrate these personal milestones. This encourages a culture where people value and celebrate each other's whole selves, not just their professional personas.

Personal Notes

Day 14 - Lead with Character, Transform Your World

"Show respect even to people who don't deserve it; not as a reflection of their character, but as a reflection of yours." – Dave Willis

In the world of leadership, the idea of "Authentic Leadership" really strikes a chord with just about everyone. This is not merely a title you hold or a role you play; it's a lifestyle that impacts every facet of your existence, both personal and professional. At the heart of authentic leadership lies strong character—a moral compass that guides you in making ethical decisions, a reservoir of courage that fuels your actions, and a core of humility that keeps you grounded. Strong character isn't just a feather in your cap; it's the cap itself. It shapes how you interact with your team, influences the culture of your organization, and extends its impact into the broader society.

Consider for a moment the ripple effect of your character on your reputation. You may have years of experience and an impressive skill set, but it's your character that people remember and talk about. If you're known for your honesty, integrity, and kindness, you'll find that opportunities come your way, not just in your professional life but also in personal relationships. Your reputation becomes an intangible asset, a form of social capital that you can't simply buy or negotiate for.

Now, let's talk about your organization. Your character doesn't just stay at the top; it trickles down, shaping the ethos of the entire organization. Employees look up to you, and your actions set a precedent for what is acceptable behavior. If you demonstrate a commitment to ethical practices and take responsibility for your actions, you cultivate an environment where trust and collaboration flourish. This, in turn, drives productivity, innovation, and long-term success.

But your influence doesn't stop at the organizational boundary; it extends into society at large. Leaders with strong character are often the ones who step up during crises, advocate for social justice, and contribute to charitable causes. In doing so, you become a role model, inspiring future leaders to also prioritize character in their leadership journey. Your actions could very well be the catalyst for positive societal change, leaving a legacy that goes beyond quarterly reports and annual reviews.

Leadership isn't just about the title on your business card or the corner office you occupy. It's about living a life so authentically that people can't help but follow you—not because they have to, but because they want to. You see, true leadership starts from within; it's built on the bedrock of strong character. That means your integrity, your courage, your humility— they're not just words; they're your lifeblood. When you're grounded in strong character, you're not just leading others, you're leading yourself, and that's where the magic happens. You become a beacon of inspiration, a pillar of trust, and a catalyst for change, not just in your workplace but in your community and even in the eyes of the world.

So let me ask you, what legacy do you want to leave behind? Because, make no mistake, your actions today are shaping the story that will one day be told about you. You've got the power right now to set the course for something extraordinary. Don't shy away from being that authentic leader who stands firm in their values, who treats everyone with respect, and who isn't afraid to do the right thing even when it's tough. **Remember, leadership isn't a role you play; it's a life you lead. And when you lead with authentic character, you don't just make a difference—you become the difference. Are you ready to step up? Because the world needs leaders like you, now more than ever.**

Three Insightful Questions to Ponder on This Topic

Do you uphold your values, even when it's tough?

Authentic leadership is rooted in consistency between what you say and what you do. If you find that you occasionally compromise your values due to external pressures, it might be time to reassess and reaffirm your commitment to those values. Every time you face a challenge, take a moment to reflect on your core beliefs and values, and ensure your actions align with them. Over time, this consistent alignment not only strengthens your own resolve but also builds trust with those around you. Remember, trust is hard to earn but easy to lose. Upholding your values, especially when it's tough, solidifies your authenticity as a leader.

How do you encourage trust and ethical behavior?

Cultivating a positive and trustful environment starts with leading by example. Regularly engage in open dialogues with your team, solicit feedback, and create opportunities for collaboration. Investing in training and workshops on ethics, communication, and team building can also be beneficial. Celebrate instances where team members exhibit ethical behavior and make it a point to address any deviations promptly and constructively. By doing so, you not only set the standard but also show that you value a culture of trust and ethics above all else.

How are you impacting society positively?

Authentic leadership extends beyond organizational boundaries. Look for opportunities to engage with your community, whether through volunteering, mentorship programs, or advocacy. Identify causes that align with your values and beliefs and contribute either through time, resources, or expertise. It's not about grand gestures but consistent, meaningful actions. By doing so, you not only make a tangible impact in society but also inspire others to do the same, creating a ripple effect. It's also essential to reflect on the long-term impact of your decisions. While short-term gains might be tempting, an authentic leader always has an eye on the legacy they're leaving behind and the broader societal implications of their actions.

Three Actionable Insights

Implement a "Blind Idea Pool":

In many organizations, ideas are often filtered through the hierarchy, which can dilute authenticity and discourage lower-level employees from speaking up. To foster authentic leadership, initiate a "Blind Idea Pool." Create an anonymous platform where employees can submit ideas for improvements, new projects, or any other aspect of the business. Periodically review these ideas in a team meeting without knowing who submitted them. This encourages unbiased evaluation and allows merit-based discussion. It also sends a message that good ideas can come from anywhere, reinforcing the importance of authenticity and character in leadership.

Develop a "Leadership Journal":

Authentic leadership is deeply rooted in self-awareness. Start a "Leadership Journal" where you regularly jot down your thoughts, challenges, ethical dilemmas, and victories. Reflect on your actions and decisions, asking yourself how they align with your core values and character. Make it a habit to review this journal periodically to identify patterns or areas for improvement. This practice not only enhances self-awareness but also helps you maintain the integrity of your character in your leadership role. Share the concept with your team and encourage them to maintain their own journals, building an environment where character is continually assessed and valued.

Initiate "Reverse Role Days":

Often, leaders become disconnected from the day-to-day challenges that their teams face, which can hinder authentic interactions. To counter this, initiate "Reverse Role Days" where leaders switch roles with employees at various levels for a day. This is not just about doing someone else's tasks but also about understanding the decisions they have to make and the ethical considerations they balance. It's a humbling experience that can reveal gaps in understanding and empathy. By stepping into someone else's shoes, leaders can gain a richer perspective, which can make their leadership style more authentic and grounded in the realities that their team faces.

Personal Notes

Day 15 - Modern Leadership

"Leadership is not wielding authority, it's empowering people." – Becky Brodin

First off, let's talk empowerment. Gone are the days when a leader's role was to sit on a high chair and dictate terms. That's a recipe for stagnant growth and zero innovation. In today's fast-paced world, you can't afford that luxury. Empowering your team not only unshackles their potential but also frees you to focus on visionary tasks. When people feel empowered, they take ownership, and let's be honest, people who own a task will always outperform those who feel 'assigned' to it. This isn't a nice-to-have; it's a must-have. So the question isn't whether you should empower your team; it's how soon can you start?

Now, let's tackle the idea of influence over authority. Have you ever inspired someone by ordering them around? Probably not. Influence is the currency of the modern leader. Your title may get you obedience, but it's your influence that will get you dedication. Influence allows you to foster an environment where ideas flow freely, and innovation thrives. The more you inspire, the less you'll have to enforce. That's not just effective leadership; it's smart leadership. Time to switch gears, don't you think?

But wait, there's more. You see, the workforce is changing, and if you're still clinging to old models of leadership, you're setting yourself up for a rude awakening. Millennials and Gen Z aren't just looking for a paycheck; they're looking for purpose, flexibility, and empowerment. They don't want a boss; they want a leader who acknowledges their aspirations and contributions. If your leadership style doesn't evolve with the changing workforce, you're not just outdated—you're obsolete.

Now, about those traditional views on leadership—authority, control, and all that jazz. Let's be critical for a moment. Those methods may have worked in an era where information was scarce and barriers to entry were high. But now? In a world interconnected through the internet and social media? Good luck with that. Trying to control everything is like trying to hold water in your hands; it's not just ineffective, it's exhausting. It's high time to drop the old perceptions that have been holding you back.

Look, I'm not just asking you to reconsider your views on leadership; I'm urging you to do it now. The world is changing, and time waits for no one. Adaptability is no longer just a competitive edge; it's a survival trait. So, are you going to step up and be the leader this new world needs, or will you stick to outdated methods and get left behind? The choice is yours, but choose quickly. The future isn't going to wait.

Listen, you've got incredible potential within you; I know it, and deep down, you know it too. But that potential is like a fire—it needs the right conditions to blaze. Leadership isn't about snuffing out that fire in others with control and authority; it's about fanning those flames! It's about empowering your team, making them see that they're not just cogs in a machine, but essential, irreplaceable parts of a grand vision. When you lead with empowerment and influence, you're not just building a team; you're building leaders, visionaries, game-changers!

Now here's the urgent truth: the world is not waiting for you to catch up. The old rulebook? Toss it. The workforce has changed, and if you're not evolving, you're stagnating. This is your wake-up call! You have an opportunity—a responsibility, even—to be more than just a figurehead. Be the leader who not only navigates the complexities of this modern world but thrives in them. **Be the leader who embraces change as a friend, not a foe. Don't just aim to keep up with the times; aim to define them! So, what's it going to be? The clock is ticking, and your moment is now. Seize it!**

Three Insightful Questions to Ponder on This Topic

How empowered does your team feel under your leadership?

Empowerment starts with trust. Begin by assessing the tasks and responsibilities you've given to your team. Are there any areas where you can provide more autonomy? Remember, the goal is not to lose control but to give them the space to express their creativity and innovation. Start with small steps: delegate projects, encourage decision-making, and seek their feedback on processes. When mistakes occur (and they will), use them as learning opportunities rather than reprimanding moments. Foster a culture of open communication where your team feels comfortable coming to you with their ideas, concerns, and aspirations. By doing so, you're not just giving them tasks; you're instilling a sense of ownership and purpose.

Are you leading by influence or authority?

Influence is earned, not given. Reflect on your interactions with your team. Are they following your guidance because they respect and trust you, or because they fear potential repercussions? Influence comes from building genuine relationships with your team, understanding their individual strengths, and aligning them with the organization's goals. Start by being more approachable. Schedule regular one-on-one check-ins, actively listen to your team members, and involve them in decision-making processes. Celebrate their successes and support them in their challenges. As you shift from a mindset of authority to influence, you'll find your team not just complying out of obligation but committing out of dedication.

How are you adapting your leadership for younger generations?

The younger generation values purpose, flexibility, and a sense of belonging. To cater to their needs, start by understanding their motivations. This might mean conducting surveys, having open dialogues, or even bringing in consultants familiar with these generational dynamics. Adapt a flexible work environment wherever possible, allowing for remote work or flexible hours. Moreover, invest in continuous learning and development opportunities, as this generation values growth and skill acquisition. Recognize their achievements in meaningful ways and create platforms for them to share their ideas and perspectives. Embrace technological advancements and social platforms, as these are second nature to them. By aligning your leadership style with their aspirations and values, you're not only retaining talent but also fostering a culture of innovation and forward-thinking.

Three Actionable Insights

Host "Impactful Storytelling" Workshops:

In a world saturated with data and metrics, the power of a compelling story often gets overlooked. Stories can inspire, motivate, and connect people in a way that no spreadsheet can. As a leader, consider hosting regular "Impactful Storytelling" workshops where team members share narratives about their professional or personal lives that have guided their work ethic, creativity, or problem-solving skills. This serves multiple purposes: it creates a culture of emotional intelligence, fosters a sense of community, and most importantly, helps individuals recognize the value of influence over mere authority.

Implement a "Reverse Brainstorming" Session:

Traditional brainstorming sessions focus on finding solutions, which is great, but what about understanding the problem at a deeper level? Initiate what's called "Reverse Brainstorming." In these sessions, instead of asking how to solve a problem, ask how you could cause it or make it worse. This technique encourages people to look at challenges from a completely different perspective and often leads to more innovative solutions. It also serves as a subtle reminder that leadership needs to evolve with the times and be open to unconventional thinking.

Launch a "Time-Capsule Project":

This is especially useful if your team or organization is going through a period of change. Have each team member write down their current views on leadership, their role in the company, and where they see the company heading. Seal these in an envelope and set a date (say, one year from now) to reopen them. In the interim, focus on implementing modern leadership tactics—empowering your team, leading through influence, and evolving with the changing workforce. When you eventually open the time capsules, it will be a powerful reflection point to see how far you've come and what old notions have been shed.

Personal Notes

Day 16 - The Power of Integrity and Character

"Integrity is doing the right thing, even when no one is watching." – C.S Lewis

What really sets a great leader apart from someone who's just got the title but not the substance? A plethora of qualities comes to mind—vision, communication skills, and adaptability, to name a few. However, at the core of enduring and impactful leadership lies an often-underestimated trait: integrity. It is not merely the titles or the charisma that define leadership; it is the indelible mark of strong character and unwavering ethical principles that separates a genuine leader from a transient one. Integrity serves as the cornerstone upon which a leader's credibility, influence, and effectiveness are built.

Let us ponder, what does a leader with integrity look like? Such a leader is uncompromising in their commitment to honesty, transparency, and fairness.

They are not swayed by short-term gains or personal benefits that come at the cost of ethical considerations. Their actions are consistent with their words, thereby engendering trust and respect among their teams and stakeholders. When leaders embody these virtues, they not only guide their organizations toward success but also contribute positively to society by setting a standard for ethical conduct.

But what happens when leaders falter in character? The repercussions are far-reaching and often devastating. History is replete with examples of CEOs and political figures who have had to step down due to ethical transgressions. Whether it's financial improprieties, harassment allegations, or other forms of misconduct, the lack of integrity not only tarnishes individual reputations but also undermines the collective morale and performance of an organization. Furthermore, these lapses in character cast a long shadow over the leader's past achievements, no matter how impressive they might have been.

So, is integrity negotiable for those aspiring to be effective leaders? The answer is an unequivocal 'no.' A lack of integrity may not manifest its consequences immediately, but it is a ticking time bomb that will eventually erode the foundations of leadership. Moreover, in an age where information is readily accessible, leaders are under heightened scrutiny, making it even more crucial for them to exhibit impeccable character. A leader's integrity serves as a protective armor in the volatile arena of public opinion and accountability.

You know, leadership isn't just about sitting at the top of the pyramid, barking out orders, and collecting accolades. Oh no, it's so much deeper than that! True leadership is about the essence of who you are, your character, and especially your integrity. Imagine being the kind of leader who walks into a room and instantly, the atmosphere changes. People don't just see your title; they feel your presence and your authenticity. They know you're someone they can trust, someone who won't cut corners or compromise on what's right. That level of trust is your superpower! It's what enables you to inspire your team to reach heights they never thought possible. Because when you lead with integrity, you're not just aiming for success; you're striving for greatness. You're building a legacy, my friend!

So, here's my challenge to you. Don't just aim to be a leader; aspire to be a leader worth following. Take those tough decisions that keep you up at night and handle them with honesty and transparency. Show up, not just in your role but in your soul. **Be the kind of leader who makes people say, "I feel better, braver, and ready to conquer the world when I'm around them." Trust me, integrity isn't just a word; it's the heartbeat of exceptional leadership. You've got this—now go out there and make your mark on the world!**

Three Insightful Questions to Ponder on This Topic

Are you true to your words and promises?

Trust is a fragile yet crucial foundation of leadership. One of the quickest ways to erode trust is by not matching your words with actions. Start by performing regular self-checks. Before making a promise or commitment, ensure you can follow through. If you find discrepancies between what you say and what you do, it's time for introspection. Are external pressures making you compromise? Or is there a lack of self-awareness? Remember, it's always better to under-promise and over-deliver. Establishing consistency takes time, but it's an investment in building genuine relationships based on mutual trust.

Do you sometimes prioritize gains over ethics?

Leaders are often faced with temptations of short-term rewards, but true leadership requires the vision to recognize the long-term consequences of these choices. Prioritizing short-term gains can be detrimental to the lasting success and reputation of both the leader and the organization. When faced with such decisions, step back and weigh the potential benefits against the long-term repercussions. Seek counsel from mentors or trusted colleagues, and consider the ethical implications of the decision. Focusing on long-term vision and ethical decision-making will not only benefit your personal leadership journey but will also ensure the sustained growth and reputation of the organization.

How often do you reflect on feedback about your leadership character?

Many leaders avoid feedback out of fear of criticism. However, embracing feedback, especially about your character, is essential for growth. Create an environment where team members feel safe to voice their opinions and concerns. When you receive feedback, instead of getting defensive, listen actively and reflect on its validity. Utilize feedback as a tool for self-improvement. If multiple individuals point out a similar area of concern, it might be an indication of an aspect you need to work on. Remember, leadership is a journey, not a destination, and every piece of constructive feedback is a stepping stone towards becoming a more effective and ethical leader.

Three Actionable Insights

Conduct "Ethical Drills":

Just like fire drills prepare teams for emergencies, "Ethical Drills" can prepare your team for moral dilemmas. Create hypothetical but realistic scenarios that challenge your team's ethical boundaries. For example, what should an employee do if they discover a colleague is fudging numbers? Discuss these scenarios in team meetings and walk through the ideal responses. It's not just about knowing what's right; it's about practicing how to act on it. This exercise will not only make ethical considerations a regular topic of conversation but also help to identify areas that may need additional training or clarification.

Launch a "Transparency Log":

While privacy and confidentiality are important, many organizational processes can benefit from more openness. Consider implementing a "Transparency Log"—a documented ledger or digital platform where key decisions, and the rationale behind them, are recorded and made accessible to team members. This includes both successes and failures. The idea is to foster a culture where decisions are made transparently, and everyone is held accountable. Over time, this practice can help build a collective ethos of integrity, as people come to understand that their actions are part of a permanent record.

Institute "Character Spotlights":

Most companies have employee-of-the-month programs focusing on performance metrics. How about one that focuses on character and integrity? Create a monthly "Character Spotlight" to recognize and celebrate employees who have demonstrated exceptional integrity or strong moral character. Whether it's an act of honesty, kindness, or moral courage, spotlighting these behaviors will not only reward good acts but also serve as a powerful reminder of the kind of conduct that the organization values. This can be done through internal newsletters, team meetings, or a dedicated section on your company intranet.

Personal Notes

Day 17 - Dual Nature of Leadership

"In the end, it's not the years in your life that count. It's the life in your years." – Abraham Lincoln

Leadership is a journey, not just a title. It's a path that many fear to tread, laden with obstacles that challenge your character, test your resolve, and question your vision. Yet, it's that very journey that shapes you into a beacon of change, influence, and impact. Leadership isn't easy; it's a balancing act. On one hand, you're at the helm, steering the ship through uncharted waters, making decisions that affect not just you but an entire team, an organization, or perhaps even a community. Every choice carries weight, and with that weight comes accountability and responsibility. The challenge is daunting, but it's in overcoming these trials that leaders are forged.

On the flip side, leadership is one of the most rewarding experiences you can ever undertake.

Imagine the gratification that comes from seeing a vision you mapped out turn into reality. Think about the lives you touch, the careers you shape, and the positive ripple effect that emanates from your actions. It's not just about charting a course; it's about inspiring others to follow you, to believe in themselves, and to strive for a collective purpose. The smiles, the thank-yous, and the visible growth of those around you are your true rewards.

What then is the true measure of success in leadership? It's not just the accolades, the financial gains, or even the milestones reached. It's the number of people you uplift, inspire, and lead towards achieving a common goal. Your real legacy isn't what you do for yourself; it's what you do for others. True leaders don't create more followers; they create more leaders.

Contrast this with the limited scope of self-centered achievement, and it's clear why leadership, despite its challenges, stands as a fulfilling endeavor. You're not just building a brand or a business; you're building people, and there's no greater accomplishment than that. Leadership is not a solo expedition but a communal effort. Your decisions will make waves, sometimes rocking the boat, but they can also set a course that leads everyone to a brighter horizon.

So step up to the challenge. Embrace the dual nature of leadership—its trials and its triumphs. Don't shy away from the hard choices and the big responsibilities. Lean into them, for it's in grappling with these complexities that you'll find your true strength. And as you rise, lift others up with you. After all, a leader is best when people barely know he exists; when his work is done, his aim fulfilled, they will say: we did it ourselves.

Leadership isn't for the faint of heart, and you know what? That's exactly why you're here, because you've got the heart of a lion. You're stepping into a role where every decision you make sends ripples throughout your team, your organization, maybe even your whole community. Sure, that sounds intimidating, but don't forget—those ripples can create waves of positive change. You've got the power to not just direct, but to inspire, to transform skepticism into belief, and to turn obstacles into stepping stones. This is your moment to shine, to show the world the mettle you're made of. The challenges? They're nothing but opportunities in disguise, chances for you to demonstrate your resilience, your ingenuity, and your ability to bring people together.

Now, let's talk rewards. I'm not talking about money or fame—although those might come too—I'm talking about the irreplaceable feeling of making a meaningful impact. Imagine looking back and seeing not just a path you've walked, but a trail you've blazed, filled with people you've guided and inspired. When you lead, you're not just aiming for success; you're aiming for significance. You have the incredible opportunity to be the beacon that lights up someone else's path, to be the catalyst in their transformation. That's what real leadership is all about. So go ahead, embrace the challenges, relish the responsibilities, and remember: your true measure isn't in the height you reach, but in the heights you help others achieve. You've got this!

Feel the energy, feel the responsibility, but most importantly, feel the immense potential that lies within you.

Three Insightful Questions to Ponder on This Topic

Are you leading for others or for your own gain?

True leadership is servant leadership. When you place the needs, growth, and development of those you lead above your personal interests, you're on the path to becoming a transformative leader. Regularly assess your motivations. If you find that your decisions are primarily self-serving, reorient your focus. Start by actively listening to your team's needs and concerns. Prioritize their growth and well-being, and you'll not only foster loyalty but also create a positive, collaborative environment where everyone thrives. Remember, the mark of a great leader is not just in the number of followers but in the number of leaders they help shape.

Do you see challenges as growth opportunities?

Your perspective on challenges largely determines your effectiveness as a leader. Every obstacle is an opportunity to learn, adapt, and evolve. Instead of shying away or getting disheartened, lean into these challenges. Embrace a growth mindset. This means believing that abilities and intelligence can be developed over time through dedication and hard work. Share this mindset with your team, fostering resilience and adaptability. When faced with challenges, gather your team, brainstorm solutions, encourage diverse viewpoints, and create a culture where mistakes are seen as learning opportunities rather than failures.

Are you a motivator or just a director?

Leadership is more than just giving orders or setting directions. It's about inspiring, motivating, and lifting others to their fullest potential. Regular feedback from your team can be invaluable in gauging how you're perceived. If you're merely directing, strive to become more inclusive. Share your vision and the 'why' behind decisions, ask for input, recognize achievements, and celebrate milestones as a team. To truly inspire, you must lead by example. Demonstrate the values, work ethic, and attitude you wish to see in your team. Encourage open communication and create a safe space where everyone feels valued. Remember, the best leaders ignite passion and purpose in others, turning visions into shared missions.

Three Actionable Insights

Run a "What-If" Scenario Day:

Leadership is about making choices and dealing with challenges. To better prepare for this, dedicate one day each month for a "What-If" Scenario Day where you and your team explore hypothetical situations that could arise in your work environment. This could range from competitive threats to internal challenges. The goal is not to create a detailed contingency plan for each, but to sharpen your team's collective decision-making and problem-solving skills. This exercise also helps team members understand the weight and impact of leadership decisions, building empathy and cohesion within the group.

Initiate a "You're the Leader" Hour:

Every week, allocate an hour where a randomly selected team member gets to be the "leader." During this hour, they get to set the agenda, lead discussions, or even introduce mini-projects or initiatives they believe would benefit the team. This not only gives everyone a taste of leadership responsibilities but also provides diverse perspectives that can rejuvenate your team's dynamics. It's an excellent opportunity for current leaders to identify emerging leadership qualities among team members, and it gives everyone a safe space to practice and understand leadership.

Launch a "Golden Feedback Loop":
Create a system where each team member anonymously writes down one thing they learned from their leader and one thing they wish the leader would do differently. Collect these insights and discuss them openly in a team meeting, without attributing comments to specific individuals. This encourages a culture of continuous improvement and transparency, and it allows leaders to gain actionable insights into their leadership style. In return, as a leader, share what you've learned from each team member and what you wish they would do differently, creating a two-way feedback loop. This practice enhances mutual growth and understanding, serving as a constant reminder of the dual nature of leadership—its challenges and its rewards.

Personal Notes

Day 18 - The Power of Appreciating Team Members in Tough Times

"Being told you're appreciated is one of the simplest and most uplifting things you can hear. "– Sue Fitzmaurice

In any organization, the cornerstone of success lies in the collective efforts of its team members. As leaders, it's easy to become engrossed in strategic imperatives and overlook the human element. But let's be unequivocal about this: the importance of appreciating your team cannot be overstated, particularly when navigating through turbulent waters. A simple "thank you" or acknowledgment can act as a powerful motivator, reinforcing the value each member brings to the table.

Human psychology is wired to respond positively to appreciation. Studies have shown that employees who feel valued are more committed, exhibit higher levels of engagement, and are more productive. During challenging times, morale often dips, and it's your responsibility as a leader to uplift your team. The act of showing gratitude can serve as an emotional buoy, stabilizing the ship when the seas are rough.

When you cultivate a culture of appreciation, the benefits ripple throughout the organization. Team members are more likely to extend the same courtesy to their peers, fostering a collaborative and supportive work environment. This collective ethos becomes your organization's competitive advantage, making it more resilient and agile, qualities that are indispensable in today's rapidly evolving marketplace.

Actioning this principle is straightforward. Make it a habit to recognize individual and team achievements in team meetings. Consider implementing a 'kudos' system, where team members can publicly praise each other for good work. If possible, tailor your appreciation to the individual, acknowledging the specific qualities or efforts that have made a difference. The goal is to make appreciation a systematic part of your leadership toolkit, not an afterthought.

The dividends of appreciating your team accrue over time, manifesting as higher retention rates, increased productivity, and a more harmonious work environment. In sum, the act of valuing your team members is not just a moral imperative but a strategic one. When you invest in the well-being of your people, you're not just building a better workplace; you're constructing a more robust and sustainable organization.

Listen, if you're in a leadership role, you've got an incredible opportunity, a privilege really, to make a lasting impact on people's lives. Don't forget, behind those spreadsheets, emails, and project plans are real humans giving their time and energy to make your vision a reality. Especially when times are tough, when the deadlines are piling up and stress levels are through the roof—that's your golden moment. Seize it! Look your team members in the eye and say, "Hey,

I see you. I appreciate you. Your work is making a difference here."

Now, I want you to think about the ripple effect that comes from that simple act of appreciation. You're not just boosting someone's day; you're laying the foundation for a culture that thrives on positivity and mutual respect. You're creating an environment where people aren't just clocking in and out; they're invested, they're engaged, and they're giving it their all. And guess what? **When your team is empowered, there's nothing you can't achieve together. So go ahead, be that leader who makes everyone around them better. Be the reason someone feels valued today. Trust me, it'll come back to you tenfold.**

Three Insightful Questions to Ponder on This Topic

How frequently do you acknowledge team efforts?

In the whirlwind of daily tasks and responsibilities, it's easy to forget the power of acknowledgment. Start by setting aside time in your calendar, even if it's just a few minutes every week, dedicated to appreciating your team members. During this time, think about each team member's recent contributions and reach out to them with specific praise. Remember, generic praise often feels hollow. Instead, identify a particular task or effort you've noticed and commend them on it. Not only does this reinforce the behaviors and actions you want to see, but it also shows your team members that you are genuinely paying attention to their work and not just going through the motions.

Have you encouraged recognition systems in your organization?

Structured appreciation systems, like a 'kudos' board or a monthly recognition event, create a consistent space for gratitude and make it a part of your organization's culture. If you haven't already, consider introducing such a system tailored to your team's dynamics. It can be as simple as a shared document or board where team members can post their appreciations or as elaborate as monthly awards or recognitions. The key is consistency; ensure that this isn't a one-time event but a sustained practice. Over time, this will build a culture where team members feel seen and valued, leading to increased morale and productivity.

Do you show vulnerability as a leader?

Authentic leadership isn't just about acknowledging your team's accomplishments but recognizing their struggles, efforts, and the emotional labor they put into their work. To truly connect and appreciate them, be vulnerable. Share your challenges, admit when you're wrong, and express genuine emotion when interacting with your team. When team members feel you relate to them on a human level, they're more likely to feel valued and understood. Hosting regular one-on-ones or check-ins where you can discuss non-work-related topics, ask about their well-being, and genuinely listen can make a significant difference in how connected and appreciated they feel.

Three Actionable Insights

Facilitate "Gratitude Circles":

Create a monthly or bi-weekly meeting dedicated solely to expressions of gratitude, which can be virtual or in-person. During these "Gratitude Circles," each team member takes turns to express what they are thankful for in the workplace and acknowledges the efforts of a colleague. This practice not only encourages gratitude but also gives everyone a moment in the spotlight for their contributions. Over time, this cultivates a work culture where appreciation becomes a social norm, boosting morale and reinforcing team cohesiveness.

Implement a "Pass-the-Baton Acknowledgment":

Designate a tangible item, like a small trophy or baton, that serves as the "Acknowledgment Baton." The idea is that the holder of the baton must pass it on to another team member within a week, along with a written or verbal acknowledgment of that person's specific contributions. The catch is that the baton must be passed to someone from a different department or someone the holder doesn't interact with daily. This creates a chain of acknowledgment that transcends departmental silos and broadens the recognition network within the organization.

Execute a "Personalized Appreciation Day":
On a rotating basis, designate one day each month to celebrate a specific team member. This isn't a birthday or work anniversary; it's a day to acknowledge that individual's contributions to the team. During this day, colleagues can share stories, anecdotes, or specific instances where the individual has excelled. To make it even more personal, tailor the day's activities or decorations to the individual's interests or hobbies. This makes the team member feel seen not just as an employee but as a whole person, thereby enhancing their emotional connection to the workplace.

Personal Notes

Day 19 - Supportive Leadership

"Surround yourself with a great team and build that team slowly. Your team is one of your most important investment and if you are careful about hiring only the best people, it will pay dividends" "– Sheila Johnson

Teamwork and good leadership are key nowadays. Gone are the days when siloed approaches and autocratic leadership styles could carry an organization to success. Today, the most prosperous companies are those that understand a fundamental truth: a team is not merely a group of individuals working in parallel, but rather a tightly-knit community founded on mutual respect, trust, and care. This shift in perspective—from viewing team members as cogs in a machine to valuing them as integral contributors to a shared vision—is the cornerstone of modern leadership.

The power of a cohesive team is exponentially greater than the sum of its parts. When team members feel a genuine sense of belonging and investment in shared objectives, the results are staggering: higher levels of innovation, efficiency, and job satisfaction. However, these outcomes are not automatic; they are the fruits of an environment carefully cultivated by empathetic and supportive leaders. Leaders who not only set high standards but also empower their team members to reach and exceed these benchmarks are the architects of success in any organization.

Let us dispel the myth that leadership is solely about making tough decisions and setting directions. True leadership is intrinsically tied to the welfare and success of the team. A leader who fails to recognize the value of their team is like a captain who ignores the condition of their ship—both are headed for rough waters. Supportive leadership is not just a managerial strategy; it is a commitment to the growth and well-being of every individual on the team. It is about recognizing that your success as a leader is inextricably linked to the collective success of your team.

It is imperative for leaders to grasp that their teams are their most valuable resources. In the modern workplace, characterized by its complexity and interdependency, a leader cannot afford to overlook the immense potential that lies in fostering a collaborative work environment. By aligning team members with a clear, shared vision and set of values, a leader can galvanize a force capable of surmounting any obstacle. More importantly, by sharing leadership responsibilities and offering consistent support, leaders can unlock untapped reservoirs of creativity, resilience, and problem-solving abilities within their teams.

Let's get real for a second. You and I both know that leadership isn't just about cracking the whip or steering the ship alone. It's about building a team that's so tight-knit, they're like family. Imagine walking into work every day knowing that you're surrounded by people who've got your back, people who are as invested in the company's dreams as you are. That's not just a team, my friend—that's a powerhouse of innovation, creativity, and resilience. And the secret sauce that binds this powerhouse? It's YOU, leading with empathy, trust, and unconditional support.

So, step up and be that leader who doesn't just see faces or roles but sees invaluable human beings. Recognize the goldmine of talent and potential that's right in front of you—your team. Lift them up, empower them, and watch how they do the same for you tenfold. **Remember, your success isn't measured by your solo climb to the top, but by how many people you bring along with you. Make it your mission, starting today, to create an environment where everyone thrives together. You've got this, and together, there's absolutely nothing you can't conquer!**

Three Insightful Questions to Ponder on This Topic

How are you building trust and respect within your team?

Trust is the backbone of every successful team. It's important for leaders to lead by example in this regard. Make an effort to be transparent in your communications, honor your commitments, and show reliability. Actively listen when your team members speak, and encourage open dialogue where everyone feels safe to express their thoughts and concerns. Consider organizing team-building activities or workshops that can help in fostering stronger interpersonal relationships. When mistakes happen, instead of resorting to blame, focus on solutions and take them as learning opportunities. Over time, your consistent efforts will build a culture of trust that benefits everyone.

How are you delegating leadership roles in your team?

Empowerment is about giving your team the tools, resources, and confidence they need to thrive. Start by ensuring that every team member clearly understands their role, the value they bring, and how it ties into the larger objectives of the organization. Provide opportunities for continuous learning and personal growth, such as workshops, courses, or mentorship programs. Celebrate individual and team achievements, no matter how big or small. When team members come to you with ideas or solutions, take them seriously and, where feasible, give them the autonomy to act. The more you show trust in their capabilities and support their growth, the more they'll feel empowered to take initiative and excel in their roles.

Are you transitioning your team from followers to leaders?

Sharing leadership doesn't mean diluting your authority; it means recognizing that leadership qualities exist in many of your team members and giving them opportunities to shine. Identify strengths within your team and delegate responsibilities that allow individuals to leverage and further develop those strengths. Establish regular feedback sessions, not just from you to them, but also from them to you. This two-way feedback loop promotes shared responsibility and mutual growth. It's also crucial to foster an environment where every opinion counts. Encourage brainstorming sessions and promote a culture where every idea is valued. By sharing leadership responsibilities and tapping into the diverse skills and experiences of your team, you're not only uplifting them but also setting the foundation for a more robust and resilient organization.

Three Actionable Insights

Introduce "Compassion Corners":

In today's high-pressure work environments, stress and burnout can be pervasive, affecting both individual performance and team dynamics. Consider introducing a dedicated space or time block called "Compassion Corners." During this time or in this space, team members can share non-work-related challenges they're facing and offer emotional support to each other. The leader participates as an equal member, not as a supervisor. This practice can significantly improve mutual respect, trust, and understanding within the team, aligning well with the principles of supportive leadership.

Roll Out "Mission Alignment Workshops":

Understanding the bigger picture can be a massive motivator. Organize regular workshops where team members can directly see how their roles contribute to the larger mission of the company. During these sessions, break down annual or quarterly objectives into smaller team-based and individual goals. Allow team members to contribute ideas on how best to achieve these smaller objectives. This participatory approach not only empowers the team but also ensures everyone is aligned with the organization's mission, thereby creating a stronger sense of shared purpose.

Implement "Role Reversal Days":

Understanding the complexities and challenges of each role within a team can breed empathy and mutual respect. Organize "Role Reversal Days" where team members swap roles or shadow a colleague for a day. This exercise allows everyone to appreciate the skills and efforts that go into each role, breaking down silos and fostering a culture of mutual respect. Leaders should also participate, either swapping roles with other team leaders or team members. Such a practice will offer valuable insights into the day-to-day challenges faced by the team, making the leader more empathetic and effective.

Personal Notes

Day 20 - The Shift from Followers to Leaders in Organizational Excellence

"The function of leadership is to produce more leaders, not more followers. " "– Ralph Nader

The best companies these days do more than just excel at their work; they also make it a priority to build strong leaders within their teams. It is crucial to understand that the quintessence of impactful leadership transcends the conventional paradigm of mere management. An effective leader is not simply an orchestrator of tasks and a manager of resources; he or she is a cultivator of nascent leaders, a catalyst for empowerment and innovation. This entails a transformative shift from a follower-centric management ethos to a leader-centric one, where the objective is not to maintain a workforce that adheres to directives, but to nurture a cadre of proactive, self-sufficient individuals capable of spearheading initiatives and making pivotal decisions.

The perils of a follower-centric approach are not to be underestimated. Organizations that rely solely on top-down decision-making are plagued with inefficiencies, stifled creativity, and diminished employee engagement. A workforce trained only to follow orders becomes a repository of untapped potential, a latent force that could otherwise contribute to the organization's adaptability and resilience. In contrast, a leader-centric approach acknowledges the latent potential in every team member and seeks to unlock it. The goal is not just to steer the ship but to create an armada of capable captains.

Integrating a culture of leadership requires a re-evaluation of organizational norms and practices. This begins with a commitment from the top echelons to foster an environment that rewards initiative, encourages constructive dissent, and facilitates continuous learning. The hallmark of such a culture is a decentralized decision-making structure, wherein power and responsibility are diffused across various levels of the organization. This flattening of the hierarchical pyramid is accompanied by an investment in leadership development programs, mentorship initiatives, and opportunities for cross-functional collaboration, aimed at equipping employees with the skills and perspective to lead.

Leadership development is not an event but a continuous process. It involves providing not just the tools and strategies but also the mindset that positions leadership as a shared responsibility. It must be embedded in the organization's DNA, intricately woven into its policies, procedures, and performance metrics. This calls for a robust system of feedback and accountability that allows for the identification and nurturing of leadership traits at every level, from front-line employees to senior executives.

You know, leadership is not a title or a position, it's a mindset, a way of living. You have the power within you to inspire, to lift others up, and to drive change. But here's the secret sauce—true leadership is not just about leading others; it's about creating more leaders.

Imagine a world where your team, your organization, isn't just looking up to you for answers but is empowered to find solutions and take charge. How liberating would that be? It's like you're not just lighting the way; you're passing the torch so that others can shine too. That's how you multiply impact; that's how you create a legacy!

Now, let's be real. Transitioning from a follower-centric to a leader-centric culture might sound challenging, but the rewards are monumental! When you invest in people, guide them, and give them the wings to become leaders themselves, you're not just building a team, you're building an empire of excellence. It's not a one-man show; it's a collective masterpiece. So, dare to take that step. Shift the paradigm. Cultivate leaders, don't just accumulate followers. Because the future belongs to those who empower others. The question is, are you ready to be that game-changer? Let's do this!

Three Insightful Questions to Ponder on This Topic

How are you cultivating an environment that rewards initiative and continuous learning?

To answer this, begin by conducting an internal audit of your organization's policies, communication patterns, and employee development programs. A leader-centric culture is evident in organizations that prioritize decentralized decision-making, encourage open communication, and actively invest in leadership development at all levels. If you find your company leaning towards a top-down approach, start by facilitating open discussions, encouraging feedback from team members, and setting up mentorship or training programs. Remember, the goal is not just to provide guidance but to empower each member to think and act as leaders in their own right.

How are you creating a space where initiative is celebrated, different opinions are welcomed, and learning never stops?

Fostering such an environment begins with self-awareness and being open to feedback. As a leader, actively seek opinions and ideas from your team, and be willing to act on them when they provide value. Ensure that your team feels safe expressing their thoughts, even if they challenge the status quo. This not only promotes innovation but also demonstrates that you value their contributions. Continuous learning can be fostered by regularly attending workshops, reading books, or participating in webinars. Furthermore, promote and facilitate opportunities for your team to do the same, emphasizing that growth is a shared responsibility.

How are you embedding leadership at all organizational levels and ensuring accountability?

Embedding leadership throughout an organization requires consistency and a strategic approach. First, set clear expectations about what leadership looks like at every level. This can be done through training, workshops, or even through clear communication channels. Encourage departments to have regular brainstorming sessions, where even the newest members are invited to share ideas and take the lead on specific projects. Implement a 360-degree feedback system, where team members at all levels are reviewed not just by their superiors but also by their peers and subordinates. This holistic approach to feedback will provide insights into leadership attributes or areas of growth. Lastly, ensure that promotions and rewards are not just based on tenure or output but also on an individual's ability to lead, inspire, and empower others. This sends a clear message about the organization's values and priorities.

Three Actionable Insights

Launch a "Solve-It Sprint" Initiative:

A "Solve-It Sprint" is a time-limited event where teams are given real-world organizational challenges to solve within a fixed timeframe, say 48 hours. It's more than just problem-solving; it's a leadership training ground. Participants are rotated through different leadership roles within the team—be it as a strategist, an implementer, or a negotiator. The rotation allows everyone to experience leadership tasks and makes room for hidden talents to emerge. Post-event, conduct a thorough debrief to discuss what worked, what didn't, and who showcased leadership qualities that were previously unnoticed.

Initiate a "Legacy Project":

Encourage each team member to initiate a "Legacy Project"—a project they would like to be remembered for during their time in the organization. It should be something that adds value but is not part of their regular job description. Provide them with a small budget, if needed, and most importantly, the autonomy to run it. It encourages forward-thinking, fosters responsibility, and lets them wear a leadership hat. At the end of the year, showcase these projects company-wide to celebrate the budding leaders and their contributions.

Implement "Office Hours for Everyone":

Typically, it's the executives and managers who hold 'office hours' for their subordinates. Flip the script. Allow every team member to host a 30-minute weekly 'office hour' where they can discuss anything from project ideas to improvement strategies. It offers two advantages: first, it empowers employees to feel like their voice and ideas matter (because they do!), and second, it encourages them to think strategically, as they now have a platform and a regular timeframe to prepare something impactful to discuss.

Personal Notes

Day 21 - Empowering Leadership

"It doesn't make sense to hire smart people and tell them what to do; we hire smart people so they can tell us what to do. "– Steve Jobs

Effective leadership is essential. The success of any organization fundamentally hinges on its ability to build and manage teams that are not just efficient, but also innovative and synergistic. However, creating such high-performing teams is not about micromanaging every task and decision. On the contrary, the most impactful leaders understand the immense value of empowering their team members, giving them the freedom to be their best selves. This hands-off yet supportive leadership style fosters an environment where each member's unique skills and perspectives can shine, contributing to the collective intelligence and capabilities of the team as a whole.

Empowerment is not about relinquishing control; it's about creating a culture of trust and mutual respect. When team members feel trusted, they are more likely to take ownership of their tasks and responsibilities, leading to higher levels of engagement and commitment. And when people are committed, they are more apt to go the extra mile, think outside the box, and contribute ideas that propel the organization forward. In essence, an empowered team is a breeding ground for innovation and excellence.

So, how does one cultivate this culture of empowerment? The first step is recognizing the innate talents and abilities that each team member brings to the table. A good leader doesn't just delegate tasks; they delegate authority and responsibility, allowing team members to make decisions that impact the outcome of their work. This not only boosts the individual's confidence but also elevates the collective decision-making capacity of the team, making it more agile and adaptive.

However, empowerment doesn't mean leaving team members to fend for themselves. A truly effective leader is always available to provide guidance, resources, and constructive feedback. They set clear expectations, but they also give people the room to experiment, learn from their mistakes, and grow. This balanced approach ensures that team members have the support they need to succeed, without feeling stifled or restricted by excessive oversight.

You've got this amazing group of people counting on you, and guess what? They're not looking for a boss to micromanage them—they're yearning for a leader who believes in them. You have the power to ignite the fire within your team, to unleash their fullest potential. Don't be the lid on their creativity; be the wind beneath their wings! Empower them, trust them, and you'll be amazed at the brilliance they bring to the table. Your team is a goldmine of untapped talents and ideas, and when you give them the freedom to shine, you're not just building a team—you're building a powerhouse!

But hey, empowering your team doesn't mean you step back into the shadows. No, you're right there, their guiding star, providing the resources, direction, and encouragement they need to soar. You set the stage for their greatness, and then you let them perform. Remember, leadership isn't about control; it's about cultivating an environment where everyone rises together. Your leadership can be that game-changing factor that turns a good team into an extraordinary one. So go out there, trust in your team's capabilities, and watch how you all break barriers and shatter ceilings, together!

Three Insightful Questions to Ponder on This Topic

Do you micromanage or trust your team's autonomy?

Micromanagement can be a result of several factors—lack of trust, fear of mistakes, or even personal tendencies of wanting to control outcomes. It's essential to introspect and understand your motives. If you find yourself leaning toward micromanagement, it may be beneficial to start practicing delegation in small ways. Begin by entrusting team members with tasks or decisions and observing the outcomes. Over time, you'll recognize the value that each individual brings and your trust in their abilities will grow. Remember, it's also okay to let them make mistakes, as this is part of their growth process. Focus on creating an environment where they can learn and evolve from these experiences.

How frequently do you offer constructive feedback and resources?

213

Providing constructive feedback is a key component of empowerment. Regularly reviewing your team's performance and offering guidance helps them align with organizational goals and personal growth trajectories. Make it a habit to have periodic check-ins with each team member, not just for feedback but also to understand their needs and challenges. Your role as a leader is not just to direct but also to facilitate, ensuring they have all they need to excel. Remember, empowerment means giving both responsibility and the tools to succeed.

How can you better appreciate each member's unique talents?

Recognizing individual talents is pivotal in creating an empowered team. Start by actively observing each member in different scenarios. Ask yourself if everyone is in a role that suits their strengths. Periodic team-building exercises or personality tests (like the Myers-Briggs Type Indicator or StrengthsFinder) can also help identify individual strengths and areas of growth. Celebrate small achievements and milestones, and make it a point to publicly acknowledge outstanding contributions. This not only boosts morale but also reinforces a culture of appreciation and empowerment. Over time, you'll see team members more invested in their roles, confident in their contributions, and eager to innovate and excel.

Three Actionable Insights

The "Human Library" Initiative:

In many organizations, team members have hidden talents, expertise, or life experiences that aren't directly related to their job descriptions but could offer valuable perspectives. Create a "Human Library" where each team member becomes a "book" on a particular subject they are knowledgeable about. Schedule short, optional "reading sessions" where team members can "check out a human book" for a conversation. This not only acknowledges the multifaceted talents within your team but also fosters cross-pollination of ideas and skills.

The "Here-and-Now" Feedback Mechanism:

Traditional feedback often happens during annual or semi-annual reviews, which may be too late to make real-time adjustments. Implement a "Here-and-Now" feedback mechanism where team members can provide instant, anonymized feedback during or immediately after meetings or project milestones. This allows the team to adapt quickly and feel that their opinions matter in real-time, thus empowering them to contribute actively to team development.

The "Skill Investment Fund":

Set aside a small budget or time allowance for each team member to invest in learning a skill of their choice, whether it's directly related to their job or not. Every quarter, have them present how they've used this "Skill Investment Fund" and what they've learned. This not only shows that you trust them to manage their own development but also instills a culture of continuous learning and personal growth.

Personal Notes

Day 22 - Transforming Toxic Workplaces

"When there is no consequence for poor work ethic, and no reward for good work ethic, there is no motivation. "– JD Roberts

In any organization, the culture is not just an abstract concept; it's a living, breathing entity that impacts everything from employee engagement to customer satisfaction. As a leader, you're not just a part of this culture; you're a key driver in shaping it. One of the most corrosive elements that can infest your workplace culture is the presence of toxic employees. These individuals can create an atmosphere of negativity, sow discord, and undermine collaboration. Tolerating such behavior not only dampens morale but can also have a ripple effect on client relationships and overall performance metrics.

You might think that one or two difficult personalities are a small price to pay for getting the job done. But here's the truth: Toxicity is contagious.

The longer you allow these individuals to operate unchecked, the more you risk normalizing their behavior. Your team members are watching you, and your actions (or lack thereof) set a precedent. When you tolerate toxicity, you inadvertently send the message that such behavior is acceptable, which can encourage a downward spiral affecting your organization's internal dynamics and its reputation in the marketplace.

You may be tempted to look for quick fixes—a team-building session here, a motivational talk there. While these interventions have their place, they are not substitutes for addressing the root cause of the issue. Ignoring or sidestepping the problem won't make it go away. And laying the blame on market conditions, competitors, or even lower-level managers is not just counterproductive; it's a failure of leadership.

So what can you do? First, take ownership. Acknowledge that as a leader, you have the power and responsibility to set the tone and expectations for your organization's culture. Next, don't shy away from difficult conversations. If someone's behavior is problematic, address it head-on. Provide clear, constructive feedback and set behavioral expectations. If there's no improvement, don't hesitate to make the tough calls—even if that means letting someone go. Your responsibility is to the entire organization, not just individual team members.

Listen, I get it; leadership isn't just a title, it's a mission—a mission to create a workplace that thrives on positivity, collaboration, and mutual respect. But let's cut to the chase: a toxic culture is the kryptonite to your super team. If you're turning a blind eye to negativity or bad behavior, you're not just damaging your team's spirit; you're putting a dent in everything you've worked so hard to build. But you know what? You have the power to turn things around, to transform your work environment into a haven of productivity and respect. Don't underestimate the impact of your actions; your team is a mirror reflecting your leadership. Be the change, set the tone, and watch your organization transform!

So, what's stopping you? Fear? Doubt? Throw them out the window! You've got a company, a team, a dream that's counting on you to step up. No more quick fixes or blaming others. Own your role, have those tough conversations, and make those challenging decisions. Your title may say "manager" or "CEO," but your actions should scream "LEADER!" **A great culture isn't built in a day, but it starts with a single decision: your decision to say "Enough is enough; we're better than this." Make that decision today, and let's unleash the incredible potential that's been waiting to burst forth from your organization! You've got this!**

Three Insightful Questions to Ponder on This Topic

Are you addressing organizational toxicity or turning a blind eye?

Ignoring toxic behavior can often seem like the easiest route, especially in the short term. Addressing it head-on requires courage, tact, and skill. However, brushing it under the carpet is a ticking time bomb. Over time, this toxic behavior can metastasize and contaminate your organization's culture, leading to a drop in morale, productivity, and overall performance. As a leader, you need to cultivate a culture of open communication where employees feel comfortable discussing their concerns. When made aware of toxic behaviors, address them proactively by initiating conversations, understanding the root causes, and implementing corrective measures. Sometimes, this might mean coaching or mentoring an employee; other times, it may involve disciplinary action. But always remember: taking action underscores your commitment to a healthy workplace, and it will gain you respect in the long run.

Are you setting behavior standards and walking the talk?

A leader's actions, words, and decisions set the tone for the entire organization. If you're inconsistent in your behavior or if you're tolerating toxic behaviors in certain situations while condemning them in others, you're sending mixed signals. This inconsistency can erode trust and can inadvertently make employees believe that such behaviors are acceptable under certain circumstances. To counter this, make sure you're clear about the values and behaviors that you want to see in your organization. Document them, discuss them in team meetings, and incorporate them into performance reviews. Most importantly, embody these values in everything you do. When the team sees their leader practicing what they preach, they are more likely to follow suit.

Do you prioritize employee well-being or just performance metrics?

Performance metrics, while crucial, are just one part of the equation. An organization's true strength lies in its people and the culture they collectively create. An emotionally healthy and happy employee is likely to be more engaged, productive, and loyal. As a leader, it's vital to recognize that behind every metric is a human being with emotions, aspirations, and challenges. By investing in the well-being of your team, not only are you boosting their morale, but you're also positively impacting the organization's bottom line. Consider implementing well-being programs, offering mental health support, and promoting work-life balance. Regular check-ins and open-door policies can also go a long way in understanding and addressing any concerns your employees might have. Remember, a thriving employee leads to a thriving organization.

Three Actionable Insights

Deploy a "Culture Ambassador Program":

Designate a select group of individuals from various departments as "Culture Ambassadors." These are people who already embody the positive attributes of your organization's desired culture. Their role will be to observe team dynamics, engage in informal conversations with their colleagues, and report back to leadership on the general atmosphere. They can also be tasked with subtly reinforcing positive behavior and discouraging negativity. To ensure that this doesn't become a "snitch program," anonymity and a focus on constructive solutions should be a cornerstone. This way, you get eyes and ears at the ground level, helping you identify toxic elements before they become an epidemic.

Conduct "Values Audits":

Too often, companies set their values in stone and forget about them. They end up becoming words on a wall rather than principles that guide behavior.

Schedule quarterly "Values Audits" where team members anonymously assess how well the company and their colleagues are living up to the stated values. Use this data to identify gaps between stated and actual behavior, especially focusing on areas that may be breeding grounds for toxicity. Once the audit is complete, share the findings and actionable steps with the team. This not only holds everyone accountable but also empowers the team to participate in shaping the organization's culture.

Launch a "Cultural Reset Bootcamp":

If you find that toxicity has infiltrated multiple layers of your organization, it might be time for a more drastic measure. A "Cultural Reset Bootcamp" is a dedicated period—say, a week—where normal operations are paused, and the entire focus is on re-aligning with the company's core values and expectations. Bring in external experts to conduct workshops, hold frank discussions about what's not working, and train team members in conflict resolution and communication skills. End the week by collaboratively establishing new norms that everyone commits to uphold. This acts as a hard reset and gives everyone a chance to start afresh, leaving toxic behaviors behind.

Personal Notes

Day 23 - Influence in a Changing World

"Leaders become great, not because of their power, but because of their ability to empower others. "– John Maxwell

The prevailing narrative surrounding leadership often paints a picture that is far from the truth— a notion that leadership is about wielding authority or instilling fear to command obedience. This archaic perspective not only fosters toxic work environments but also stifles innovation and personal growth. Think about it: when was the last time you were inspired to give your best under the shadow of fear or authoritarian rule? Likely, never. Leadership is not a dictatorship. It's high time we debunk this myth and embrace a more enlightened understanding of what true leadership entails.

What sets a remarkable leader apart is not the ability to instill fear, but the capacity to empower, inspire, and motivate a team to unlock their fullest potential.

A people-centric approach is not just another buzzword; it's the cornerstone of effective leadership. When a leader focuses on developing individual strengths, acknowledging efforts, and creating an environment where everyone feels valued, the results are transformative. People are not just cogs in a machine; they are the machine. Empowering them equips your organization with a powerful engine that can conquer even the most challenging terrains.

It's not your title or your ability to enforce rules that make you a leader. It's your influence. Influence fosters an environment where ideas are free to grow, and innovation becomes the norm. When people follow you because they want to—not because they have to—you've achieved the pinnacle of leadership. Influence motivates people to take action not out of obligation, but out of a genuine belief in a shared vision. This is the essence of a leader who uses influence over authority, and it's a game-changer in any organizational setting.

We are living in a world marked by rapid changes—technological advancements, a diversified workforce, and an increasingly competitive landscape. The old rulebook on leadership is not just ineffective; it's obsolete. A shift in perception is not an option but a necessity. The leaders who will thrive in this new world are those who adapt and align their strategies to a more collaborative and inclusive model. The stakes are high, and the time for change is now.

Leadership is not a destination but a journey—a journey toward creating a culture that thrives on empowerment, values influence over authority, and is agile enough to adapt to an ever-changing world. If you are a current or aspiring leader, or someone interested in organizational development, consider this your call to action. Discard the outdated beliefs that have held you and your teams back. Step into a new era of leadership that doesn't just aim to command but seeks to inspire, empower, and transform. The future is waiting, and it looks bright for those willing to lead the way.

You've probably heard that leadership is all about wielding authority and keeping people on a tight leash—forget that! That's a relic of the past, a misconception that's done nothing but build walls between us. True leadership, the kind that leaves a lasting impact, is about empowering people, including yourself, to become the absolute best versions of themselves. When you focus on lifting people up rather than pushing them down, you're not just a boss—you're a beacon of inspiration!

Don't get caught up in the old ways of thinking that leadership is a one-person show, about flexing your muscles and instilling fear. No, no, no! It's time to pivot, friends! We're in an ever-changing, hyper-competitive world, and if you want to thrive, you've got to adapt. Lead with influence, not with authority. Create an environment where everyone, from the intern to the executive, feels they have the freedom to speak up, innovate, and contribute to the greater good. **Remember, the best leaders aren't those who stand in the spotlight, but those who make sure the spotlight shines on everyone. Now go**

out there and be the leader the world needs—
you've got this!

Three Insightful Questions to Ponder on This Topic

Are you leading by authority or influence?

Analyzing your own leadership style requires an honest assessment of how you interact with your team. If you find that your decisions are typically top-down, without seeking input or feedback from your team, you might be leaning too heavily on authority. On the other hand, if you prioritize listening, engaging team members in decision-making, and value the unique perspectives they bring, you are leading with influence. Remember, influence creates a collaborative environment where team members are more motivated to contribute and innovate. To transition from authority to influence, start by creating open communication channels, encourage team feedback, and actively involve them in decision-making processes. Foster an environment where every opinion is valued, and recognize the efforts of those who actively contribute.

How are you empowering and fostering innovation in your team?

Empowerment begins with trust. To encourage innovation, you need to allow your team members the freedom to think outside the box, take risks, and occasionally make mistakes. Create a safe environment where mistakes are viewed as learning opportunities rather than failures. Regularly invest in training and development programs to upskill your team. Recognize and reward innovative ideas and encourage brainstorming sessions. Listen actively to their suggestions and give them ownership of projects or tasks where they can lead and shine. The more autonomy and trust you give, the more they'll be motivated to exceed expectations.

Is everyone in your team feeling heard and valued?

A healthy organizational culture promotes inclusivity and diversity, recognizing that every individual brings a unique perspective that can be invaluable. To ensure everyone feels valued, regularly seek feedback from all levels of the organization—not just the top tiers. Organize team-building activities to promote camaraderie and understanding. When disagreements arise, approach them with an open mind and encourage constructive dialogue. Hosting regular town-hall meetings or open forums can also provide a platform for voices that might otherwise go unheard. If you identify areas where inclusivity is lacking, address them head-on and make necessary changes. Remember, a leader's role is to serve their team, and by ensuring everyone feels heard and valued, you're laying the foundation for a more cohesive and productive work environment.

Three Actionable Insights

Institute "Problem-Solving Power Hours":

Every month, allocate an hour where team members can freely discuss challenges they're facing, without judgment or immediate repercussion. The catch? The focus should be on actionable solutions, not just airing grievances. To ensure this doesn't turn into a complaint session, involve a neutral facilitator who keeps the discussion on track. Team members can submit topics anonymously beforehand, which the facilitator will present. The goal is to collaboratively find solutions and have leadership commit to at least one action item at the end of each session.

Implement "Culture Scorecards":

Incorporate aspects of organizational culture into regular performance evaluations. Create a scorecard that includes key attributes that reflect the culture you want to build—like teamwork, positivity, and respect for others. This shouldn't be a tool for punitive action but rather a constructive guide for personal development. Employees and managers can use these scorecards during one-on-one meetings as a structured way to discuss strengths and areas for improvement related to workplace culture.

Roll Out a "Sustainability Stewardship" Program:

Work culture and external societal values are increasingly interconnected. Implement a program where each department takes turns spearheading a community service project or sustainability initiative each quarter. This not only promotes teamwork but also aligns the company with broader values of social responsibility. It gives team members a sense of purpose that goes beyond the workplace, fostering a positive culture by unifying people under a shared, meaningful mission.

Personal Notes

Day 24 - Real Leadership

"In times of adversity and change, the true character of a leader is revealed. "– James Lane Allen

The notion of leadership is often conflated with power, status, or public image, it's crucial to revisit the foundational elements that constitute "Real Leadership." At its core, true leadership is inseparable from good character. It's not merely a role you assume when you step into the office or stand in front of a team; it's a life you lead every single day. Your actions, both public and private, paint a vivid picture of your character, serving as a living example to those you seek to lead. A quick scan of recent headlines will reveal CEOs who have resigned or faced public backlash, not necessarily for their lack of professional skills but for questionable character.

You might wonder, why does character hold such weight in leadership? The answer is straightforward yet profound: A leader with integrity, empathy, and humility garners trust. When your team trusts you, they are not just following a boss; they are following a human being who stands as a moral and ethical compass. In difficult times, this trust becomes the glue that holds the team together, enabling you to navigate challenges with collective resilience.

Think about it—would you be inspired to follow someone who is incredibly skilled but lacks a moral foundation? The likelihood is slim. Skills can be taught, strategies can be learned, but character is cultivated over a lifetime. If you lead with authenticity, your team will recognize and respect your genuine self, making you not just a good leader but an exceptional one.

However, it's essential to understand that good character doesn't imply perfection. Everyone has flaws; what sets a real leader apart is the willingness to acknowledge them. By being open about your vulnerabilities, you not only humanize yourself but also encourage a culture of openness and growth within your team. After all, the most potent form of leadership is leading by example.

Listen, I get it—leadership can feel like a heavy crown on your head, filled with responsibilities and expectations. But let me tell you, real leadership isn't about the title on your business card or the number of followers you have on social media. No, my friend, it's about the unshakeable character that forms the core of who you are. It's about being someone others can trust, not because you say the right things, but because you do the right things. Your character is your compass, and when you lead with integrity, honesty, and respect, you're not just a leader in name—you're a leader in action. You become someone who lights the path for others, who inspires people to believe that they too can become better versions of themselves.

So, if you're aiming to be a leader, start by looking inward. Ask yourself, "Am I the person others can count on?" If the answer is anything less than a resounding yes, then it's time for some soul-searching.

Don't just aim to be a person of success; aim to be a person of value. Remember, skills can be taught, but character—that's what sets you apart. So go ahead, be your authentic self, and let your character shine. **When you lead with your truest self, you're not just making a difference; you're setting the stage for a legacy. And that, my friend, is what real leadership is all about.**

Three Insightful Questions to Ponder on This Topic

Do you routinely reflect on your actions aligning with your values?

Regular self-reflection is crucial for growth and personal development, especially for leaders. Set aside some time each week for introspection. Review your actions, decisions, and interactions. Ask yourself if they align with your core values and the principles you hold dear. If discrepancies arise, it's an opportunity for growth. Being honest with oneself is the first step to improvement. Consider keeping a journal to track your reflections and any action plans to address areas of growth. By committing to regular self-evaluation, you nurture both personal and leadership development.

How do you handle character challenges and ethical dilemmas?

Every leader will face moments when their character is tested. It's not just about the decision you make but also about how you arrive at that decision. When faced with challenging situations or ethical dilemmas, take a step back and evaluate all potential outcomes, not just in terms of business results but also in terms of integrity and morality. Engage in open dialogue with trusted advisors or mentors who can offer insights and guidance. Your response to these challenges will shape your reputation and demonstrate to your team the values you truly uphold. Remember, it's in the difficult moments that real character shines through.

How are you promoting openness, integrity, and growth?

Creating an environment where team members feel safe to voice their opinions, acknowledge their mistakes, and seek growth is a hallmark of strong leadership. Start by leading by example: be transparent about your own vulnerabilities and mistakes, and show how you learn and grow from

them. Encourage feedback loops within the team –
perhaps through regular team meetings or one-on-one
sessions. Praise and reward not just results, but also
the process and integrity behind achieving those
results. Consider implementing training sessions on
ethics, communication, and leadership to further
instill these values within your team. Lastly, always
emphasize that mistakes are opportunities for learning
and growth. When your team sees this in action,
they'll be more inclined to embrace these values
themselves.

Three Actionable Insights

Conduct "Character Check-ins":

Regularly take time to assess your character and how it aligns with your leadership style. Schedule half-hour slots every month to sit down alone or with a trusted colleague to evaluate your actions, decisions, and how they reflect your core values. Ask yourself questions like, "Have I been fair and honest in my dealings? Have I compromised my integrity for expediency? How can I improve?" This routine helps you remain conscious of your character and its impact on your leadership. You can even have a list of character traits that you and your team value the most and rate yourself on those.

Initiate "Ethos Challenges":

To put the focus on character, introduce monthly "Ethos Challenges" within your team. These are small, real-world challenges designed to exercise specific character traits such as empathy, courage, or fairness. For example, one challenge could be to resolve a long-standing conflict with a colleague or another could be to admit a mistake openly and take corrective action. At the end of the month, offer a platform for team members to share their experiences, without any judgment or repercussions. This not only strengthens individual characters but also fosters a culture of character-based leadership within the team.

Launch "360-Degree Character Reviews":
Unlike regular performance reviews that focus solely on job performance and skills, these reviews include assessments on character traits as they relate to leadership. Involve not just superiors but also peers and subordinates in providing anonymous feedback on your character. Questions could range from ethical conduct to interpersonal respect. Take this feedback seriously, and work on actionable steps to improve. This practice encourages a culture where character is valued as much as competence.

Personal Notes

Day 25 - Empathy for Transformative Leadership

"The strongest people are not those who show strength in front of the world but those who fight and win battles that others do not know anything about "– Jonathan Harnisch

In a world that often prioritizes efficiency, bottom lines, and quick results, we sometimes overlook the integral human element that serves as the backbone of our organizations: the emotional well-being of our employees. I've witnessed first-hand the corrosive effects of a lack of empathy in leadership. Leaders devoid of emotional intelligence might boast impressive resumes and even deliver short-term results, but their inability to connect with their team on an emotional level creates an environment of disengagement and fear. When people in power are blind to the personal struggles that their employees endure—whether it's a family crisis, addiction, or other significant life challenges—they miss out on opportunities to build a truly cohesive and motivated team.

Let's pause and consider the spectrum of personal issues that employees might be navigating on any given day. Imagine Jane, a project manager, who just lost her father but is back at work after only a week off. Or consider Ahmed, a junior developer, quietly battling addiction. These are not isolated cases; they are daily realities that deeply affect job performance and emotional well-being. Employees like Jane and Ahmed don't need a boss who simply allocates tasks; they need a leader who can recognize their emotional states, offer genuine support, and adapt expectations accordingly.

To lead effectively, it's not enough to merely pay lip service to the idea of a "supportive work environment." It requires actionable steps: open-door policies, regular check-ins, and a company culture that encourages vulnerability and dialogue rather than punishing it. When employees feel safe sharing their issues, they're not just happier; they're also more productive, engaged, and loyal to their organization. A leader who fosters this environment isn't just being altruistic—they're making a sound business decision.

The importance of cultivating this kind of workplace cannot be overstated. In my years of consulting with various organizations, I've found that teams led by empathetic leaders are more adaptive, innovative, and ultimately, successful. Employees are more willing to go the extra mile for a leader who shows them genuine respect and kindness, because they feel seen and valued. Remember, a team is a reflection of its leadership. If the leader is cold and insensitive, this will cascade down, creating an environment where employees feel disposable and undervalued.

Listen up, because this is crucial: Your title might say 'Manager,' 'CEO,' or 'Team Lead,' but what you should really aspire to be is the Chief Empathy Officer of your workspace. Understand this—people don't care how many degrees you have or how many companies you've led to success until they know how much you care about them. We're all fighting battles that aren't visible; it could be a tough family situation, mental health struggles, or other personal challenges. Your role as a leader is to create a sanctuary at work, a place where your team feels safe, heard, and valued. That's how you build a team that would walk through fire for you—by first walking through fire for them.

And let me hit you with some real talk: Kindness and empathy aren't just fluffy buzzwords; they're the secret sauce to skyrocketing your leadership game to legendary levels. Imagine a workplace where everyone feels like they can bring their full selves to the table, where they're not just cogs in a machine, but integral, respected parts of a thriving community. That's the kind of work environment that breeds innovation, commitment, and yes, skyrocketing success. **So go ahead, be that beacon of empathy and understanding. Show your team the respect and kindness they deserve, and watch how they transform not just your business, but also you, into something extraordinary.**

Three Insightful Questions to Ponder on This Topic

Are you attuned to your team's personal challenges or just their work?

Understanding your team's emotional well-being goes beyond recognizing their professional skills or accomplishments. Start by initiating one-on-one conversations where you actively listen to their concerns, feelings, and challenges. Be present and resist the urge to jump to solutions immediately. Sometimes, merely being heard can be therapeutic for the employee. Once you gain insights into their lives, you'll be better equipped to offer support or resources, whether it's flexible hours, professional counseling, or just an empathetic ear. By demonstrating genuine concern, you not only elevate their well-being but also build trust, which is invaluable in a team dynamic.

Do you encourage vulnerability and open dialogue?

An atmosphere of trust is vital for fostering vulnerability. Encourage team meetings where personal check-ins are routine. Perhaps start by sharing some of your own challenges, which can set a precedent for others to open up. When someone does share, refrain from being judgmental or dismissive. Implement and promote open-door policies, and ensure there are no repercussions for those who speak their minds. Consider providing training or workshops on emotional intelligence and communication skills. As vulnerability becomes a norm, you'll find that not only do team members feel more connected and understood, but they'll also be more collaborative and innovative in their work.

Are you proactive in understanding and supporting your team's emotions?

Being reactive means you're often playing catch-up, and opportunities to support your team may be missed. Instead, be proactive. Schedule regular check-ins, even if it's just a brief chat over coffee. Conduct anonymous surveys to gauge the emotional well-being of your team. Invest in training that focuses on empathy, active listening, and emotional intelligence. By being proactive, you demonstrate that the emotional well-being of your team is a priority, not an afterthought. This not only boosts morale but can also lead to increased productivity and loyalty.

Three Actionable Insights

Introduce "Empathy Roundtables":

Once a month, organize a gathering where team members can openly discuss topics related to emotional well-being, personal challenges, and workplace dynamics, all while maintaining confidentiality and respect. The leader should act as a facilitator but mainly listen. This allows employees to feel heard and gives management invaluable insights into the lives of their team members. Over time, these Empathy Roundtables can become a safe space for everyone to share and support each other, solidifying the team's bond.

Implement "Impactful Pause Moments":

Encourage team members to take a brief moment before meetings, project launches, or decision-making sessions to acknowledge the human element involved. This could be as simple as asking everyone to share one good thing that happened to them in the past week or something they're grateful for. The idea is to slow down and consider the emotional state of everyone involved, recalibrating the group's focus toward empathy and emotional intelligence.

Roll Out "Personal Passion Projects":
Allow employees to spend a small portion of their work time (say, 10%) on a project that aligns with their personal interests or passions but also adds value to the team or organization. The leader should take an active interest in these projects, providing resources and moral support. This practice not only boosts morale and job satisfaction but also allows the leader to understand the individual strengths and interests of their team members, which can be leveraged for future projects.

Personal Notes

Day 26 - Proven Strategies for Transformative Impact

"Great leaders are not the best at everything. They find people who are best at different things and get them all on the same team " - Eileen Bistrisky.

When I first stepped into a leadership role, I quickly realized that it wasn't just about titles or authority. It was an honor, a privilege granted to me. To you, the emerging leaders reading this, understand this: leadership is not an entitlement; it is a gift. It's a chance to make a difference, to leave an indelible mark. Treat this privilege with the respect and gratitude it deserves.

I've sat in countless meetings, listening more than speaking. Why? Because true leadership isn't about dominating conversations; it's about fostering collaboration. Listen to your team, value their insights, and together, you'll craft solutions far greater than any one person could conceive. It's not about being the loudest in the room; it's about ensuring every voice is heard and valued.

Pause for a moment and reflect on the leaders who've made a difference in your life. The weight of their impact is profound, isn't it? Now, as you step into those shoes, approach your role with reverence. Recognize the ripple effect of your decisions, your actions, and your words. Leadership isn't just about guiding; it's about influencing with integrity and respect.

At the heart of every decision, every strategy, is a person. As leaders, our primary role isn't just to achieve goals but to inspire and develop those we lead. I urge you to look beyond the numbers and see the faces, the dreams, and the potential. Lead with empathy, and your team will follow with passion.

I've always believed in the impossible, and as a leader, it's my mission to instill that belief in my team. Dream big, encourage bigger. Every morning, remind your team of the mountains they can move, the stars they can reach. Your belief in them will become their fuel, propelling them to become the best versions of themselves. Remember, a leader's true success is measured not by their achievements, but by those they inspire.

Leadership isn't just about guiding a team or making decisions; it's about awakening the dormant potential in others, about lighting the path to greatness. Remember, true leadership is a journey, not a destination. It's a journey of self-discovery, of understanding your unique purpose and the profound impact you can make. Every morning you wake up, you hold in your hands the incredible opportunity to change lives, to inspire, and to leave a legacy.

But leadership also demands courage. The courage to challenge the status quo, to dream bigger, and to stand firm in the face of adversity. As you embark on this transformative journey, always remember: you are not alone. Surround yourself with those who believe in your vision, who uplift and challenge you. And in moments of doubt, when the path seems uncertain, look within and draw strength from the knowledge that you are destined for greatness. **Lead with heart, with purpose, and let your actions inspire others to reach for the stars.**

Three Insightful Questions to Ponder on This Topic

How are you ensuring inclusive decision-making?

Effective leaders create an environment where every team member feels comfortable sharing their perspectives without fear of judgment. Begin by actively inviting input from everyone, especially those who tend to be quieter. Schedule regular feedback sessions, and consider implementing open forums or brainstorming sessions where the primary goal is to gather ideas. Actively practice active listening; this means fully concentrating, understanding, and responding to what is being said, rather than just passively hearing the message. By valuing and integrating the insights of all team members, you not only make better-informed decisions but also foster a culture of trust and inclusivity.

How do you balance goal attainment with inspiring your team?

Balancing goal achievement with people development is at the heart of effective leadership. Start by setting clear and measurable objectives for your team, but pair them with individualized growth plans. Invest in your team's professional development by offering training, mentorship, and opportunities for advancement. Recognize that every member of your team has unique strengths and aspirations, and take the time to understand them. Celebrate not just team milestones, but personal growth achievements as well. By aligning individual passions and strengths with organizational goals, you'll find that both can thrive in tandem.

How brave are you in challenging the status quo?

Leadership often involves stepping out of one's comfort zone and facing resistance. It's vital to cultivate a support network. Surround yourself with mentors, peers, or even external networks that understand your vision and can offer advice, perspective, or simply a listening ear. Remember that every great change in history faced opposition initially. Draw strength from your convictions and the understanding of why the change is necessary. Additionally, keep a journal or some form of documentation that charts your journey, the reasons behind your decisions, and the outcomes. This can serve as both a personal reflection tool and a source of motivation during challenging times. Lastly, continuously communicate your vision, reinforcing its benefits and the positive impact it will have, ensuring that as many people as possible are aligned with your direction.

Three Actionable Insights

Institute "Visionary Vision Boards":

Encourage team members to create a vision board that captures their personal and professional aspirations. This visual representation acts as a constant reminder of what they're working towards.

Schedule a team-building session where everyone crafts their own vision board using magazines, print-outs, and personal photos. Provide the materials and a space for creative expression. Once completed, allocate a space in the office for these boards or encourage digital versions for remote workers.

This exercise not only boosts motivation but also allows team members to understand and appreciate the aspirations of their colleagues, fostering a deeper sense of camaraderie and shared purpose.

Initiate "Collaborative Creativity Days":

Set aside dedicated days or hours where team members come together, not for regular work tasks, but to brainstorm and collaborate on new, out-of-the-box ideas without the constraints of their usual roles.

Once a month, have a "Creativity Day". Divide team members into mixed groups, ensuring that individuals from different departments come together. Pose a broad question or challenge and let them brainstorm solutions or new ideas.

This initiative not only fosters innovation but also promotes cross-departmental understanding and collaboration. Over time, it can lead to unexpected and groundbreaking ideas that benefit the organization.

Establish "Legacy Ladders":
Encourage every team member to think about the legacy they want to leave behind in their role, no matter how big or small. This promotes a long-term mindset and a focus on meaningful impact.

Implementation: Host a workshop where team members reflect on their desired legacy within the organization. Have them list out actions they can take to achieve this. Periodically, revisit these "Legacy Ladders" to gauge progress and recalibrate.

Benefit: When individuals think about their long-term impact, they're more likely to invest deeply in their roles and make decisions that benefit the organization in the long run.

Personal Notes

Day 27 - Resilience and Personal Growth

"Life is 10% what happens to us and 90% how we react to it." - Charles R. Swindoll

Every journey, whether personal or professional, is paved with challenges and roadblocks. However, it's essential to understand that these are not dead ends but rather detours guiding us towards personal growth. Life is not about avoiding storms but learning how to dance in the rain. Every setback you encounter is not a sign of failure but a lesson waiting to be learned. Embrace these lessons, for they are the stepping stones that lead to greatness.

Take a moment to reflect on the last time you faced a significant challenge. Did it break you, or did it make you stronger? Often, it's our reactions to these situations that dictate our path. Instead of viewing them as insurmountable obstacles, view them as opportunities to grow, learn, and evolve. By shifting our perspective, we can transform even the most formidable challenges into valuable experiences.

Remember, imperfection is the shared thread that binds us all together. It's in our mistakes that we find our true selves, and it's in our struggles that we discover our strengths. You are not alone in your journey, and every person you meet is fighting a battle you know nothing about. Extend compassion to yourself and others, understanding that we are all works in progress, each carving out our unique paths.

Affirm to yourself that you are capable of great things. Do not let setbacks define you. Instead, let them refine you. With every challenge you overcome, you're not only proving your resilience to the world but also to yourself. Take pride in your journey, knowing that with every twist and turn, you're becoming a stronger, wiser, and more capable leader.

Life's journey is not a straight path, but rather a winding road filled with ups, downs, twists, and turns. Every challenge you face, every setback you experience, is a testament to your strength and resilience. It's natural to feel overwhelmed at times, but remember, it's these very moments that shape us. They don't come to break us but to teach us, to mold us into the best versions of ourselves. Embrace these lessons, for in them lies the secret to true personal growth and transformation.

Now, take a deep breath and reflect on your journey so far. Each scar, each tear, each memory holds a story — a story of perseverance, determination, and growth. You are not defined by the number of times you've fallen, but by the countless times you've risen, stronger and wiser. Your attitude towards challenges is your greatest weapon. **So, equip yourself with positivity, see every obstacle as a stepping stone, and march forward. Remember, it's the climb that shapes the peak. Embrace your journey, for it's shaping a magnificent you.**

Three Insightful Questions to Ponder on This Topic

How have past reactions to setbacks shaped your growth?

It's imperative to recognize that every challenge, no matter how significant or trivial it may seem, offers a chance for reflection and growth. Begin by taking a step back and evaluating your reactions to past setbacks. Were you quick to give up? Did you see them as learning opportunities? By understanding your previous responses, you can identify patterns that either aid or hinder your progress. For future challenges, aim to approach them with a mindset of growth and learning. Instead of letting emotions like fear or disappointment dominate, channel them into determination and resilience. Remember, it's not about avoiding the storm but learning to navigate through it.

When have setbacks defined you, and how can you reframe them?

It's human nature to occasionally feel defeated by setbacks or to dwell on our imperfections. However, holding onto these moments too tightly can limit our potential. Start by listing instances where you've felt defined by a mistake or setback. Next, for each instance, identify what you've learned or how you've grown since that time. This exercise will help shift your perspective from viewing these events as defining moments to seeing them as refining moments. By embracing your imperfections and setbacks as tools for refinement, you open up a world of growth, understanding, and self-compassion.

How are you fostering a positive attitude towards challenges?

Cultivating a positive attitude requires intentional practice. Begin by surrounding yourself with positive influences, be it books, podcasts, mentors, or friends who uplift and inspire you. Daily affirmations can also be instrumental in shaping a more optimistic mindset. Each morning, remind yourself of your strengths and capabilities. When faced with a challenge, instead of viewing it as a deterrent, see it as an opportunity for growth. Visualization techniques can also be beneficial – imagine overcoming the challenge and focus on the sense of accomplishment you'd feel. Equip yourself with knowledge and skills relevant to your field or passion; being prepared can often mitigate feelings of overwhelm. Lastly, remember to be kind to yourself. Understand that setbacks are a part of the journey, and every experience contributes to your unique story and personal growth.

Three Actionable Insights

Launch "Resilience Workshops":

Embracing challenges and setbacks is easier said than done. Host periodic "Resilience Workshops" where team members can share their stories of overcoming adversity in both personal and professional spheres. By creating a safe space for such discussions, employees can derive inspiration from their colleagues' experiences. These workshops can be complemented with resilience-building exercises, role-playing scenarios, and expert-led sessions on coping strategies. Over time, these sessions will not only help individuals bounce back from setbacks but will also foster a resilient team culture.

Institute "Growth Reflection Retreats":

Sometimes, all one needs is a little time and space to reflect and recharge. Organize quarterly or biannual "Growth Reflection Retreats" where employees can disconnect from their routine tasks and engage in introspective activities. These retreats can be a mix of individual reflection time, group discussions, and guided activities that help individuals recognize their growth areas. Such retreats provide an opportunity to identify learning moments from past challenges, set growth-oriented goals, and develop actionable plans to achieve them.

Implement "Resilience Recognition Awards":

While it's common for organizations to recognize top performers, it's equally crucial to acknowledge those who've demonstrated remarkable resilience. Create a "Resilience Recognition Award" to celebrate employees who've turned challenges into learning opportunities and showcased personal growth in the process. This recognition can be based on peer nominations, where team members highlight colleagues who've exemplified resilience in specific situations. By celebrating resilience, you send a powerful message about the value of growth-mindedness and the importance of bouncing back from adversity.

Personal Notes

Day 28 - The Transformative Power of Inspirational Leadership

"Don't underestimate the value of having a good team! You don't become successful on your own. You have to rely on really good people. " - Alicia Quarles

Leadership is not just a position or title; it is a profound responsibility that beckons the heart and soul. Every individual you lead carries a reservoir of untapped potential, a treasure trove of gifts waiting to be discovered. You, as a leader, have the esteemed privilege—and indeed, the responsibility—to unearth these latent talents, to shine a light on them and watch them illuminate the world. When you truly believe in your team and invest in their growth, you're not just building a workforce; you're crafting a legacy.

Imagine a world where every leader recognized the boundless potential in their teams, where collaboration wasn't just a buzzword, but the very essence of success. Such a world isn't just a dream—it can be our reality. But it starts with you. You must be the torchbearer, the visionary who sees beyond the present and into the vast possibilities of what could be. Your belief in your team's capabilities can elevate them, inspiring them to reach heights they never thought possible.

Yet, leadership is also a mirror. It reflects who you are, your values, and your aspirations. As you stand at the helm, guiding your team towards greatness, take a moment to reflect. Are you merely directing, or are you truly leading? Are you harnessing the power of collective genius, or are you stifling it? Dive deep into introspection, and understand that every decision you make, every word you utter, has the power to uplift or diminish.

The mantle of leadership is heavy, but it is one that can be worn with grace, passion, and unwavering belief. You are more than just a manager or a supervisor; you are a beacon of hope, a pillar of strength, and a catalyst for change. Your team looks up to you, not just for direction, but for inspiration. Your faith in them can move mountains, and your guidance can chart unexplored territories.

Each one of you has the power to be more than just a figurehead or a name on a door. Leadership, in its truest essence, is about recognizing the boundless potential that resides within every member of your team. It's about seeing beyond the surface, beyond the daily tasks and routines, and acknowledging the vast reservoir of talent, passion, and dreams waiting to be tapped. Remember, every individual you lead is a universe of possibilities. And as a leader, you are the compass guiding them, the spark that ignites their flame, and the wind beneath their wings. Embrace this role, not as a burden, but as the most profound privilege.

But this journey isn't just about them—it's about you too. Every step you take, every decision you make, reflects your values, your vision, and your belief in the potential of others. When you invest in your team, when you believe in their dreams as fervently as they do, you are not just building a successful enterprise, but you're crafting legacies, stories that will be told for generations. **So, stand tall, lead with passion, and remember: your belief in someone can be the bridge between their aspirations and their reality. Be that bridge. Be that leader.**

Three Insightful Questions to Ponder on This Topic

Is leadership to you about authority or genuine influence?

Leadership is far more than the power or authority vested in a title. It's an opportunity to have a positive impact on people's lives. Start by regularly assessing your motivations and actions. Are they geared towards personal gain or the collective growth of your team? One effective way to align with the latter is by investing time in understanding each team member's strengths, aspirations, and challenges. By creating an environment where everyone feels valued and heard, you not only boost morale but also harness the collective strength of diverse talents.

Are you introspective about your leadership impact?

Introspection is a powerful tool for personal growth and effective leadership. Regularly set aside quiet moments to reflect on your actions, decisions, and their impacts. Consider feedback, both positive and negative, as a means to understand how you are perceived. Remember that your actions and words set the tone for your team. If you promote open communication, trust, and continuous learning, your team will likely mirror these values. Always strive to be a role model, demonstrating the values and behaviors you wish to see in your team.

How are you tapping into your team's potential and believing in them?

Every individual brings a unique set of skills, experiences, and perspectives to the table. As a leader, it's crucial to recognize this diversity and leverage it for collective growth. Dedicate time to have one-on-one conversations with your team members, understanding their aspirations and providing opportunities for them to grow and shine. Encouraging continuous learning and offering platforms for them to showcase their talents can significantly boost confidence and productivity. Your unwavering belief in them can be a driving force, pushing them to overcome challenges and achieve excellence. Celebrate their successes, and more importantly, stand by them during setbacks, providing guidance and assurance.

Three Actionable Insights

Initiate "Perspective-Shift Workshops":

These workshops are designed to help team members and leaders step into each other's shoes. The aim is to foster understanding, build empathy, and shed light on the diverse challenges and opportunities that different team members face. By experiencing the roles and responsibilities of their colleagues, individuals can develop a deeper appreciation for the myriad of skills and talents within the team.

Once a month, arrange for team members to swap roles or responsibilities for a day or half-day. Following the swap, host a debriefing session where participants can share their insights, learnings, and newfound appreciation for their colleagues' roles.

Such exercises can break down silos, enhance team cohesion, and foster a holistic understanding of the organization's operations. It also amplifies the importance of every role and helps in recognizing the inherent value each individual brings to the table.

Roll Out "Strengths Spotlight Sessions":

These sessions focus on identifying and celebrating the unique strengths and talents of each team member. Instead of focusing on weaknesses or areas of improvement, the emphasis is on what each individual excels at and how that can be leveraged for team success.

On a bi-monthly basis, select one or two team members to be in the "spotlight". During a team meeting, discuss and highlight their strengths, past achievements, and how their unique abilities have contributed to the team's success. Encourage peer recognition during these sessions.

This practice boosts morale, enhances individual confidence, and fosters a positive work environment. It serves as a reminder that every team member, with their unique strengths, plays a pivotal role in the collective success of the team.

Launch "Holistic Health Initiatives":

Recognizing that the well-being of employees is multidimensional – encompassing physical, mental, emotional, and spiritual aspects – this initiative aims to promote holistic health among team members.

Organize monthly workshops or sessions focusing on different dimensions of well-being. This could include mindfulness meditation sessions, financial well-being workshops, or even group physical activities like yoga or hiking. Encourage team members to share their own practices or routines that contribute to their holistic health.

A holistically healthy team is more engaged, motivated, and productive. By investing in the comprehensive well-being of team members, leaders not only show they care but also ensure a more resilient and vibrant workforce.

Personal Notes

Day 29 - Purpose, Passion, and the Power to Transform

"The role of a creative leader is not to have all the ideas; it's to create a culture where everyone can have ideas and feel that they're valued. " - Sir Ken Robinson

Today, there's a clear demarcation between managers and leaders. A manager, as the text illuminates, may excel in overseeing tasks and monitoring performance. But a true leader? They soar beyond the mundane. Leaders ignite passion, inspire their teams, and drive them towards unparalleled excellence. While a manager ensures the job gets done, a leader ensures that the job done is transformative, pushing boundaries and redefining standards.

Dive into the world's most successful companies, and a common thread emerges - a thriving organizational culture. The text paints a vivid picture of such enterprises where employees aren't just mere cogs in a machine. They are valued, nurtured, and inspired. These companies don't just retain talent; they cultivate it, enabling individuals to evolve into the best versions of themselves. It's not about clocking in hours; it's about fostering a culture where aspirations meet opportunities.

When one thinks of engagement in the workplace, monetary incentives often spring to mind. But the text offers a refreshing perspective. The best companies, the real game-changers, achieve high levels of employee engagement not just through financial rewards but through a deeper, intrinsic connection. Employees in these organizations aren't just working for a paycheck; they are zealously dedicated because they resonate with the company's ethos, its purpose, and its overarching goals.

Purpose isn't just a buzzword; as emphasized in the text, it's the lifeblood of true leadership. Leaders don't merely set goals; they breathe purpose. They don't just lead teams; they inspire them, serving as living embodiments of the values they espouse. In the hustle of targets and deadlines, it's easy to lose sight of the bigger picture. But true leaders, as described in the text, always anchor their actions in purpose, ensuring that every endeavor is not just about achieving an objective but about making a difference.

In life, there's a profound difference between just 'doing' and truly 'leading'. Every one of us has the potential to be more than a cog in a vast machine, to rise beyond mere task completion and truly inspire. Remember, leadership isn't about titles or hierarchies; it's about igniting passion, fostering a culture of collaboration, and making a genuine difference. It's about understanding that every task, no matter how small, is a step towards a greater purpose. And as you embark on this journey, know that it's not the managerial skills, but the heart and purpose you pour into every endeavor that truly transforms.

Dive deep into the essence of leadership. Embrace the challenges, cherish the learnings, and always strive to elevate not just yourself, but everyone around you. Because when you lead with purpose and passion, you don't just achieve targets, you touch lives. **Remember, in the grand narrative of your career, don't just be someone who did their job; be the beacon that others aspire to follow. Stand tall, lead with heart, and watch as the world transforms around you.**

Three Insightful Questions to Ponder on This Topic

How do you distinguish between managing and leading passionately?

To navigate the transition from being a manager to a true leader, you must first understand the fundamental differences between the two. A manager often focuses on tasks, deadlines, and ensuring that processes are followed, while a leader concentrates on the 'why' behind these tasks. Begin by clearly defining your team's purpose, aligning their roles with the larger goals of the organization. Engage with your team on a personal level, understanding their aspirations, strengths, and areas of growth. Focus on fostering an environment of trust, inspiration, and continuous learning. Remember, leadership is not about directing; it's about guiding, inspiring, and enabling. Communicate with clarity and enthusiasm, ensuring that your team feels a sense of belonging, purpose, and motivation to exceed not just for the company's success but for their personal and professional growth.

How are you cultivating a value-driven organizational culture?

Building a thriving organizational culture begins with understanding and embodying the core values of the company. Once you've grasped these values, you must weave them into the fabric of daily operations and interpersonal interactions. Start by acknowledging and celebrating the achievements of your team, no matter how small. Open channels of communication, encouraging feedback and fostering a culture where innovation and fresh ideas are welcomed. Organize team-building activities, workshops, or seminars that emphasize the importance of collaboration, trust, and shared goals. Moreover, provide ample opportunities for professional growth, be it through training, mentorship, or cross-functional projects. Remember, a vibrant organizational culture is one where employees feel seen, heard, and motivated by a shared purpose.

How do you ensure purposeful leadership amidst deadlines?

Anchoring leadership in purpose amidst the pressures of the corporate world requires clarity of vision and unwavering commitment. Start by defining your personal 'why' and aligning it with the organization's overarching goals. When setting targets or introducing projects, always provide context – ensuring that your team understands the broader impact of their efforts. During challenging times, instead of solely focusing on the numbers, emphasize the larger mission and how achieving these targets plays a pivotal role in realizing the shared vision. Remember to lead by example; demonstrate resilience, positivity, and commitment to the purpose in all your actions and decisions. By doing so, you'll inspire your team to approach their tasks with the same lens of purpose and passion, even when under pressure.

Three Actionable Insights

Initiate "Future Visioning" Workshops:

A "Future Visioning" workshop involves team members envisioning the future of the company, project, or team in the mid and long-term. This is an exercise in strategic foresight where individuals tap into their imagination to visualize what success looks like down the line.

Monthly or quarterly, gather your team for a dedicated session. Ask them to think about where they see the organization in 3, 5, or even 10 years. Use tools like storyboarding, scenario planning, or even simple vision boards. Encourage them to think beyond metrics, considering aspects like company culture, societal impact, and innovations.

This practice not only fosters a forward-thinking mindset but also instills a sense of collective ownership and alignment towards a shared vision.

Establish "Diversity and Inclusion Think Tanks":

A "Diversity and Inclusion Think Tank" is a dedicated group within an organization focused on brainstorming and implementing strategies to ensure a diverse and inclusive work environment.

Assemble a diverse group of individuals from different departments, levels, and backgrounds. Meet bi-monthly to discuss the current state of diversity and inclusion in the organization, identify areas of improvement, and brainstorm actionable steps. This group can also host guest speakers, organize workshops, and create resources for the broader organization.

Such an initiative ensures that diversity and inclusion aren't just buzzwords but are actively integrated into the fabric of the organization, leading to richer perspectives and a more inclusive environment.

Roll Out "Purposeful Project Pitches"

"Purposeful Project Pitches" are opportunities for team members to pitch project ideas that align with the company's purpose, values, and long-term vision.

Create a platform or a dedicated time slot where team members can present their ideas, not just from a business or profit perspective, but in terms of alignment with company values and societal impact. These pitches can be evaluated based on feasibility, alignment with company vision, and potential impact. The best pitches can be given a green light for execution.

This approach not only fosters innovation but also empowers employees to think in terms of purpose and long-term value, reinforcing the importance of alignment with company ethos.

Personal Notes

Day 30 - Altruism and Generosity

"We rise by lifting others. " - Robert Ingersoll.

In our daily lives, materialism often overshadows our true purpose, lies the golden thread of altruism and generosity. True happiness, an emotion so profound yet elusive, doesn't stem from the transient satisfaction of possessions, but from the immeasurable joy of giving. It's a truth, as timeless as existence itself, that when we extend our hand in kindness, we don't just lift another; we elevate our own spirit.

Leadership is more than just a title or a position. It's a responsibility, a calling to shine a light so bright that it inspires others to find their own. True leaders are those who serve, who dedicate themselves to unlocking the potential within others. Because leadership isn't about standing above; it's about lifting others higher, making them believe in the magic within themselves. Remember, every time you help someone believe, you're not just creating a follower; you're cultivating a new leader.

Our journey towards personal growth and fulfillment is intrinsically tied to our acts of kindness. With each benevolent gesture, we don't just change someone's day; we evolve, inching closer to our highest selves. This growth is not just a journey of self-discovery, but a realization of an abundance mindset. For in abundance, we see that there's enough for all, enough love, enough success, enough joy. And in this realization, we are set free.

It needs to be said, and said again: the riches of the heart are unparalleled. The universe has an uncanny way of returning the goodness we put out, often manifold. When we give, not expecting in return, we receive the most precious of all – a heart full of gratitude, love, and purpose. This isn't a mere belief; it's the unwavering truth of existence.

At the crux of our existence, standing tall are the pillars of leadership and kindness. Every act of generosity, every moment of leadership, echoes in eternity, leaving behind ripples of positive change. It's through these acts that we truly live, finding purpose and meaning. For in the end, it's not about how much we have, but how much we give; not about how high we rise, but how many we uplift. And as we walk this path, let us remember and reiterate: true fulfillment lies in service, in leadership, in love.

In this journey called life, we often chase after the tangible, believing that our worth is measured by what we possess. But I urge you to look deeper, to recognize the boundless power of altruism and generosity. Remember, it's not the weight of our wallets, but the depth of our hearts, that truly defines us. When you lead with compassion, when you give selflessly, you don't just enrich the lives of others; you elevate your own spirit to heights unimaginable.

Embrace the true essence of leadership. It's not about standing at the pinnacle alone, but about lifting others to stand beside you. **Each act of kindness, each gesture of generosity, ignites a spark that can** illuminate the darkest corners. As you journey forward, let this be your guiding light: Lead with heart, give without expecting, and watch as the universe unfolds its magic in your life.

Three Insightful Questions to Ponder on This Topic

Are you shifting from personal gain to selfless service?

Transitioning from a materialistic mindset to one that values altruism and generosity requires both introspection and action. Start by evaluating your current beliefs and values. Ask yourself why certain material possessions are important to you. Often, we attach value to things because of societal pressure or personal insecurities. Reflect on the moments when you felt genuinely happy and fulfilled. More often than not, these are moments connected to relationships, personal achievements, or acts of kindness, rather than acquisitions. To actively cultivate a generous spirit, begin by setting aside a portion of your time or resources for charitable acts. This doesn't always mean monetary donations; it could be volunteering, mentoring, or simply helping a neighbor. Over time, you'll find that the joy derived from these acts far outweighs the temporary happiness of material gains.

How are you growing genuine leadership qualities and inspiring others?

True leadership is rooted in service and empathy. Begin by understanding and valuing the strengths and aspirations of those around you. Invest in their growth by providing opportunities, feedback, and, most importantly, your time. Remember that listening can often be more powerful than speaking. By actively listening to the needs and concerns of others, you show them that you genuinely care. Leadership is also about setting a personal example. Demonstrate integrity, resilience, and commitment in your actions, and others will naturally look up to you. Regularly challenge yourself by stepping out of your comfort zone, and encourage others to do the same. This creates an environment of mutual growth and trust.

Are your acts of kindness driven by sincerity or recognition?

Authentic acts of kindness stem from empathy and a genuine desire to make a difference. To ensure your acts are genuine, it's essential to regularly check in with your intentions. Ask yourself why you are choosing to help. Is it to feel better about yourself, to gain recognition, or because you genuinely care about the well-being of the other person? Remember that true generosity does not seek the spotlight. You can practice this by occasionally performing anonymous acts of kindness. This allows you to experience the pure joy of giving without expecting anything in return. Over time, this cultivates a habit of selfless giving, where the act itself becomes its own reward.

Three Actionable Insights

Institute "Kindness Kudos":

Implement a system where team members can publicly acknowledge acts of kindness and generosity demonstrated by their colleagues. This not only encourages a culture of gratitude but also emphasizes the importance of altruism in day-to-day tasks.

Action Steps:

- o Set up a physical "Kindness Board" or a digital platform where people can pin notes of appreciation.
- o Dedicate a few minutes in weekly meetings for team members to share their "Kindness Kudos."
- o Encourage leaders and managers to lead by example by actively participating and acknowledging acts of kindness they've witnessed or experienced.

Launch "Leadership by Listening Sessions":

Encourage leaders to hold regular sessions where they simply listen to their team members. The aim isn't to solve problems immediately but to truly understand the perspectives, challenges, and aspirations of others. This promotes a culture of empathy and underscores leadership as a service.

Action Steps:

o Schedule regular sessions where team members can sign up to share their insights without the pressure of immediate problem-solving.

o Ensure that these sessions are free from interruptions and that the leader actively listens without immediately jumping to solutions.

o After the session, leaders can reflect on the conversations and determine if and how they can assist or implement changes based on the feedback received.

Facilitate "Generosity Journals":

Encourage team members to maintain a journal where they record acts of generosity they've undertaken, witnessed, or been the recipient of. This serves as a personal reflection tool and a reminder of the impact of altruistic actions in the workplace.

Action Steps:

- o Provide team members with physical journals or digital platforms to record their observations.
- o Organize monthly "Generosity Gatherings" where team members can voluntarily share stories from their journals.
- o Recognize and celebrate consistent journal keepers, not for the number of entries, but for their commitment to recognizing and promoting generosity.

Personal Notes

Embracing the Leadership Horizon

And so, dear reader, we come to the end of this 30-day journey, but in many ways, this is just the beginning. Over the past month, you've delved deep, confronted challenges, and emerged with a clearer vision of the leader you aspire to be. The pages of this book might have a final chapter, but your leadership journey is an ongoing narrative, filled with limitless possibilities and potential.

Each day, you've taken steps, some big and some small, towards elevating your leadership. Remember, it's not about the grand gestures but the consistent, intentional actions that culminate in genuine change. It's the commitment to growth, the embrace of feedback, and the humility to know that leadership is a path of continuous learning.

As you move forward, carry with you the lessons, reflections, and insights gained from these 30 days. But also remember that leadership is an evolving process. The world changes, you change, and the dynamics of leadership transform with time. Stay adaptable, stay curious, and most importantly, stay true to your core values and beliefs.

There will undoubtedly be challenges ahead, moments of doubt, and times when the path seems uncertain. But with the foundation you've built and the tools you've acquired, you are more than equipped to navigate these complexities. Embrace them, for they are the crucibles that will further refine and define your leadership prowess.

I want to leave you with a thought: Leadership is not just about leading others; it's about leading oneself with authenticity, purpose, and passion. Continue to elevate, inspire, and make a difference. Your journey doesn't end here; it takes flight. Soar high, lead with conviction, and let the world witness the magnificence of your leadership. Your journey through these pages has been a shared odyssey of growth, learning, and transformation.

If the insights and strategies within have resonated with you, I invite you to share your reflections. Your feedback not only elevates others on their leadership path but also fuels our collective journey of growth. If you feel inspired, please take a moment to leave your thoughts on the Amazon book page. Let's continue to uplift, empower, and inspire one another.